MODERN HANDBOOK
OF
ELECTRONIC LIBRARY SYSTEMS

MODERN HANDBOOK OF ELECTRONIC LIBRARY SYSTEMS

CHERIAN MATHEW

CYBER TECH PUBLICATIONS
4264/3, Ansari Road, Daryaganj, New Delhi-110002 (India)
Ph.: 011-23244078. Fax: 011-23280028
E-Mail: cyberpublicationsdelhi@yahoo.com

Modern Handbook of Electronic Library Systems

First Edition 2011

Published by G.S. Rawat

For Cyber Tech Publications

4264/3, Ansari Road, Daryaganj, New Delhi-110002

Ph.: 011-23244078. Fax: 011-23280028

E-Mail: cyberpublicationsdelhi@yahoo.com

Printed at Asian Offset Printers 9212182454

Contents

Preface

Traditional library system is going sea-change under the impact of recent developments in the field. Digitalisation and automation are the order of day.

The present book imparts highly useful information on different library systems, currently in usage. The valuable information is gathered under the following headings in this book—Introduction; Automated Acquisition System; Automated Collection Management Systems; Systems Study; What is Systems Design?; Automated Serials System; Effects of Technology on Library Staff; Challenge of Information Materials Preparation; Flow Charting: As a Tool; Automated Circulation System; Censorship, Intellectual Freedom, and Collection Development; Appendices; Glossary and Bibliography etc.

The information is supported by fact and figures derived from research findings of leading library professionals from all across the world. Definitely, this work will prove vade mecum to all library professionals besides academics, trainers and trainees in the field.

We express our gratefulness to all those men of letters whose works are cited or substantially made use of herein. The real credit this ought go to them all Our teachers, colleagues and friends have rendered yeoman's service by way of guidance, inspiration and assistance. We are deeply indebted to them also. Finally we appreciate our publishers for evincing keen interest in this project and materialising it elegantly in the present shape.

Suggestions and comments for improving the contents of this are welcome from all quarters which we will incorporate in subsequent edition with due acknowledgement.

—Author

1

Introduction

> "The real tragedy of life is not in being limited to one talent, but in the failure to use the one talent."
>
> —*Edgar W. Work*

In the modern age of information technology, libraries are transforming to electronic library or digital library.

We will elucidate library systems in the context of modern libraries.

First we have to understand what a system is?

A lexical definition of a system is "an assemblage of objects united by some form of regular *interaction* or *interdependence*." This definition implies dynamic processes consisting of interrelated functions that tend to become increasingly complex as the volume or requirements placed on a system grows.

What are Library Systems?

Broadly conceived the library functions in the framework of two major types of systems: the data processing and the informational. The data processing system may be defined as the organization and the methods involved to perform operations necessary to effect the form or content of information needed to satisfy the library's *management requirements* and goals. The informational system may be defined as the organization and the methods followed in storing and retrieving information to satisfy the library's *service require-ments* and goals. Generalizing the distinction between the two major types of systems, the data processing system is concerned with the manipulation of data (clerical functions) and the informational system with the storage of information and its recovery.

It is a significant to note that a more specific level six basic systems can be identified within the library. All contain the characteristics of the data processing and informational systems previously defined. Some of these belong almost completely in one category, while others consist of a combination of data processing and information storage and recovery. Considering its predominant function of ordering and receiving library materials and paying and accounting, the functions of the *acquisitions system* depend mainly on data processing operations.

Likewise the *serials control* system is heavily concerned with data processing functions from which, however, an informational system evolves that permanently stores serials information for future reference. The *circulation control* and the *library administration and planning* systems are examples of the combination of the data processing and the informational systems. The major function of the circulation system is the control of the flow and movement of library materials.

The function of the administrative system is that of organizing and controlling the operation of the library as a whole, receiving the reports and statistics of each of the other systems and summarizing and analyzing this information to make meaningful decisions and to determine whether management goals are being served. The *cataloguing system*, with an appreciable amount of data processing, is primarily an informational system charged with classifying books and other library materials and providing the records essential for retrieving them.

The *reference system* also may be regarded as an informational system, concerned as it is with retrieval and transfer of information required by the library user.

Essentials of a System

It is pertinent to note that, in any type of system will be found four basic elements: the input, storage, processing and output components.

That these four components are present in any system is demonstrated by a random illustration of input, storage, processing and output of the human "nervous system": *input,* finger touches a hot stove; *storage,* the impulse arrives at the brain where the previous experiences of the system as a whole are stored; *processing*, the brain sorts out the questions asked of it and transfers these to a pain signal; *output* the pain signal triggers the removal of the finger from the stove.

Basically, we can consider the data processing and informational systems referred to as the two major types in a library. The data processing system contains these four elements: the *input element;* the *memory element* (storage), or unit, where information is stored until it is ready to be processed; the *processing element* where the various calculations necessary to transactions are made; and finally the *output element* where the desired results are obtained or action occurs. It will be recognized that these four elements in data processing are identical to those found in a computer system. The informational system is almost identical to the data processing system in the generalized view.

It too contains the *input* unit or clement by which information is received; the *memory* unit (storage) where the information is held until desired; and the *output* unit. There is no need for the *processing* unit. The information is required with no manipulation or change.

In fact, formation and use of the traditional library card catalogue illustrate the operation of an informational system. The inputs are the cards prepared and field by the cataloguing department and the memory and storage unit is the file in which the catalogue cards are stored. In this example the output element (the catalogue card) is not activated until a reader approaches the system, the card catalogue, with a need for information on a specified subject, thus generating an input that is his need for information.

The informational system cycle is continued: the reader locates in the catalogue the desired information—output— that the book wanted is in the library and that it carries a specific location number.

Subsystems

Remarkably, model of an acquisition system serves as an example for analyses of interrelated functions within a system. The figure shows the combination of all the components required to make this acquisitions system operational. Within this or any other system there is always a group of interrelated subsystems, each of which is designed for the performance of a particular task. This acquisitions system model consists of the subsystems *preorder search*, *ordering, receiving, checking, accounting* and *reporting*.

The sub-systems depend one on the other for input and output to fulfill specified requirements. For example, the order subsystem could not operate alone; it requires the verified information (output) supplied by the preorder search subsystem. The operation of checking in books carries with it the function of comparing the on-order slip with the book when it is received.

A decision is made on whether or not the book and the on-order slip correspond. If they do not, action is taken so that the slip and the book are referred to the order subsystem for review and follow-up. If the two do correspond, the resulting action is the property stamping of the book and its being forwarded to the cataloguing system for further processing.

Operations of a System

Here we must note that each subsystem consists of a group of logically interrelated operations. Each operation is concerned with the performance of certain functions, or certain decisions, or both, as the bases of action.

For example, the preorder search subsystem may consist of the following illustrative elements:

Operations

Searching library records

Searching trade bibliographies and other sources of title verification

(*a*) *Functions*

Verification of title

Provision of order information

(*b*) *Decisions and Actions*

Decision: Is item in collection?

Yes...........No............

Action: Duplicate............Do not duplicate............

Decision: Is item available? Yes............No..............

Action:	Order...............Not order...................
Decision:	Information sufficient to satisfy ordering subsystem? Yes.................No.................
Action:	Order Refer to requestor for additional information...........

Thus we can see that the *operations,* which are the major elements of the subsystem, consist of specified *functions, decisions,* and *actions,* also known and referred to as *elements of operations*—the basic "building blocks" of a system and its subsystems. In an effort to clarify the meaning of and relationships among these elements the following explanations are offered:

(*a*) *operations*—processing;

(*b*) *functions*—the substance of processing, that is, the objectives;

(*c*) *decisions*—the questions to be answered in the course of the processing; and

(*d*) *action*—action taken as a result of the decision.

Practically, consistency of approach in the study of each system based on these elements reveals the interaction among operations in all systems of the library organization.

Total Systems

There is no system in which the operations are isolated within a single subsystem. Characteristically, as illustrated, it will be found that there is a direct as well as an indirect effect on the operations of another system and its subsystems. It is the complexity of this interaction between and among systems that is causing libraries to investigate the concept of "total systems" before automating any operation when undertaking a systems study. When synthesized and coordinated, the six basic library systems comprise what may be termed the "total library system" or the library functioning as an entity.

It is the combination of these systems, with well–defined operational interrelationships and recognition of information transfer requirements among them, that assures effective and efficient operations directed toward achievement of the total system's, the library's overall established goals. Integration is necessary to facilitate exchange of significant information on a need-to-know basis among system comprising the total system. A total system is one in which traditional departmental boundaries tend to fade and artificial separations find no place. The total systems concept is not new in library administration but its full application beyond acknowledg-ment of it through a broadly functional organizational structure has been hampered and, indeed, prevented by the absence and unavailability of technological aids for a job that has always been overwhelming—the storage and controlled use of the mass of "data" native to the library.

The use of modern business methods for processing and storing the varied, accumulating and ever-changing data generated and used by the library would appear to be a requirement in the medium-to-large-sized library. The total systems concept is more completely and successfully implemented in terms of preciseness and timeliness of needed information through machine methods, than by laborious, economically unjustified, and error-prone manual methods. To be sure, reference personnel in evaluating the library's collection can hand produce subject area lists for analysis.

More probably such lists will be generated by merely scanning the shelf list under main classifications, resulting in an imprecise, generalized conclusion regarding the improvement of the collection. On the other hand by using data generated by the acquisitions and cataloguing departments and stored in computer memory the reference personnel can study this storage to obtain accurate and detailed information and then use their time applying the professional judgement necessary for valid collection evaluation.

Examples of the high utility of the computer in applying the total systems principle can be multiplied. Circulation control based on the data stored in the computer by acquisitions and cataloguing becomes more precise and timely and can be programmed for ready analysis of collection use and reader characteristics. This can be done manually but the results are likely to be reported too late and at too great a cost to be useful in improving currently chronic service deficiencies.

The principle that has led to the application of the total systems concept is that of monitoring and feedback. In a total system feedback is the relaying of information from one system to another, so that a given system can adjust to satisfy the requirements of the total system. For example if the demand for books in a particular subject area is increasing, this is evidenced in the circulation system's records.

In a computer based system the information in these records would be monitored. When demand exceeds predetermined criteria, management would be notified for the purpose of taking appropriate action. Therefore planning of individual systems is not done in isolation. Such planning should always be in the context of developing a total system giving maximum service to readers and eliminating duplication of staff effort.

Library Data Processing System

Obviously, the complexity of any data processing system prohibits analysis, evaluation and design as a one-step process. The job of the study staff in the analysis phase of the data processing system is that of identifying the major activities of the system, the *subsystems*.

The subsystems together satisfy one or more secondary requirements or demands placed on the system and contribute to the satisfaction of the system's primary requirements. With the subsystems identified the operations occurring within the subsystem can be isolated and the functions and decisions associate with the manipulation of each input needed to prepare the desired output can be defined.

Finally the required actions resulting from the various decisions also can be defined. The level of detail in such an analysis as this depends on the type of system being developed. If the design of a computer system is contemplated, the functions and decisions must be defined in sufficient detail to permit a programmer to programme the system.

The total system operates within an environment dictated by the goals of its parent organization or governing body.

"The first consideration in the total systems concept is description of its objectives. They can be simply stated as: (*a*) to organize administrative work flow from the viewpoint of the [library] as a whole, without regard for barriers of organizational segments; and (*b*) to develop data processing systems whereby source data are recorded once and thereafter perpetuated in various summary forms to meet departmental operating and financial needs, without repetitive processing."

In fact, the realization of the total system concept occurs when the major operating systems have been so designed and integrated that the interaction and exchange of information are facilitated in a logical and systematic manner. The planning of individual systems is not an end in itself. Such planning must always be in the context of developing a total system of reciprocal relationships among individual systems. This requires the design of integrated procedures, taking into account all of the library's systems.

No doubt, the cost of punched card equipment, or computer equipment, or both, and the extent to which this equipment can profitably be put to use for any library requires planning for the future. The total systems concept can be adapted to limited use of machines for appropriate operations within a system or for all operations in one or several systems. The urgency is that a systems study be oriented toward a future goal and that the six basic library systems be tested, reviewed, and designed to that all can perform as a whole. The decision to use machines is an administrative one and depends on all the factors that determine the role of any one library. Although a computer-based total systems goal may be a good administrative objective, the systems study could be hampered by the question of the administration's economic ability. It is now generally realized that computer use rarely saves money.

It is more important to recognize that proper use of the special talents of professionally trained librarians is essential to handle the proliferating volume of literature to be controlled, so that the users can be more profitably served. If machines are not the answer for a small library, the study should result in the design of operations in order that clerical processing can be done by other than the professional staff members who will then be free to render the creative and imaginative service appropriate to their professional qualifications.

Now we will discuss two important steps in automated library systems, which every library professional should posses

KEY WORD SEARCHES

The Wilson and Information Access indexes discussed in the previous chapter are of the subject heading or controlled vocabulary type. The advantage of such an indexing method is that it solves the problem of synonyms (*e.g.*, "Death penalty", "Capital punishment") and variant forms of expression (*e.g.*, "Fraudulent advertising", "Advertising, fraudulent")—because of the principle of uniform heading it groups together under one term works that treat the same subject but refer to it by different words. This grouping function saves you the considerable trouble of having to look in a wide variety of places for material on one subject. But there are corresponding disadvantages to a controlled vocabulary system. First, the grouping function is sometimes achieved at the expense of blurring fine distinctions between subjects. One reader, for example, was interested in the idea of "patients actively participating in the therapeutic process".

The LC subject heading that includes material on this topic is "Patient compliance"—which is not quite the same thing as "active patient participation". Still, it is close enough that the catalogers apparently decided to use it rather than to create a new heading. Another example is provided by the researcher who wanted material on

"Subfractional horsepower electric motors". I showed her the *LCSH* heading "Electric motors, Fractional horsepower", but she insisted that she wanted only subfractional and *not* fractional. When we looked at the cards under the "Fractional" heading, however, we saw that it included works on subfractional motors. Evidently, the catalogers, seeing no separate heading in the list for "Subfractional", simply chose the closest heading that did exist.

This often happens. *Distinctions that are important to subject specialists may not be perceived as important by library catalogers; and if you want to retrieve library materials you must think in the terms used by the catalogers, not the subject specialists. LCSH* headings thus often include subjects that are not precisely indicated by the terminology of the heading.

Second, a controlled vocabulary system frequently cannot get too specific within one subject. This is particularly true of the card catalogue, which seeks to summarize the content of works as a whole (*i.e.*, the principle of co-extensivity, rather than indexing individual parts, sections, or chapters of a book).

Thus the researcher who was looking for material on the dental identification of Hitler's deputy Martin Bormann could find a general heading on "Bormann, Martin, 1900—", but not a precise one on "Dental identification of Martin Bormann". Similarly, a researcher looking for "Effects of wing design on reducing heat stress at supersonic speeds in military aircraft" will not find a controlled vocabulary term that is nearly as precise as he would wish.

The whole idea of such a controlled system is to create *groups* of records; and groups by their very nature have to have more than one item in them. Third, controlled vocabularies are also by nature rather conservative and slow to change. The main reason for this is that a cataloger cannot simply insert a new term into the list without integrating it with the existing terms through a web of cross-references that must extend from the new word to the others and *to* the new word from the others, with broader/narrower relationships defined in both directions. This takes considerable effort and so catalogers are cautious about acting too quickly—they find it is often advisable to wait until the new subject comes to standardize its own vocabulary first. And so if your subject is in a new field, or is of recent development, its terms may not yet appear in the system. An example is provided by Leon Festinger's groundbreaking book *A Theory of Cognitive Dissonance* which opened up a whole new field of psychology.

It was not until several years later that the precise term "Cognitive dissonance" became a fixed subject heading in the vocabulary of *Psychological Abstracts—thus* for a time the literature of a developing field was not easily accessible. Fourth, the cross-reference structure of a controlled vocabulary system may not be adequate to get you from the terms you know to the beading that is acceptable. For example, *Psychological Abstracts* has always indexed articles on the psychological problems of hostages released by terrorists; but a few years ago (prior to the phenomenon's becoming relatively common) its thesaurus of subject headings did not include cross—references from the terms "Hostages" or to the subject heading that it uses instead.

The problems for researchers, then, are these: What do you do when there is no subject heading that corresponds to what you want to find? Or what do you do when the cross-references are inadequate to lead you to the heading that does exist somewhere in the list? So far we have seen two methods of circumventing such limitations of controlled vocabularies: you can look for likely *titles* rather than subject headings, as they may be more precise; and you can systematically browse materials arranged in a subject classification scheme. Both methods work for books, but they involve a lot of hit-or-miss searching. And neither works for journal articles, as citations to these are not accessible by title within conventional indexes, nor are the articles themselves arranged in logical groupings on the shelves.

But there are a number of unconventional indexes that can solve the problem of there being no subject heading for what you want. The three most important of these are:

1. *Science Citation Index (1955—)*; quarterly with annual and five-year cumulations. This huge index covers over 3000 journals in all fields of science, plus another 3000 nonscience journals insofar as they have science-related articles. (It should be noted, though that for the ten years 1955—1964 many fewer journals are indexed—coverage in the thousands extends only from the mid- 1960s to the present. A further note: while citation searching is possible from 1955 to date, the key word index first appears in 1966).
2. *Social Sciences Citation index* (1966—); quarterly with annual and five-year cumulations. This provides complete coverage of about 1500 journals in all fields of the social sciences, plus selective coverage of about 4500 others in sciences and humanities.
3. *Arts & Humanities Citation Index (1975—)*; published three times a year with annual and five-

year cumulations. This provides cover to-cover indexing of over 1300 journals in its broad fields, plus selective coverage of the science and social science journals insofar as they have humanities articles (*e.g.*, papers on electronic music in the technical journals).

All three are published by the Institute for Scientific Information (ISI in Philadelphia.

It is remarkable that issue of an ISI index, whether quarterly, annual, or five-year cumulation, is itself a multivolume set consisting essentially of a "Pennuterm" Subject index, a Source index and a Citation index. The first of these is an alphabetical list of all significant or key words from the titles of all journal articles covered by that issue and arranged in such a way that if you look up one word you can tell if any other word of interest appeared with it in the title of an article. This allows for great precision in searching. For example, one reader looking for articles on "Managing sociotechnical change" had a problem with the conventional indexes because no subject heading reaches this concept efficiently—the "Management" term in *LCSH* covers too wide a field. However, with the *Social Sciences Citation index* (or *SSCI),* the reader could look up the precise word "sociotechnical" to see if it appears with the words "managing" or "management" in the title of someone's journal article.

It does—there are at least ten hits that are right on the button. Similarly, a researcher interested in "the administrative position of the Captaincy in colonial Brazil" couldn't find a precise enough *LCSH* heading; however, with the ISI indexes he could look up "Captaincy" to see if it appears with "Brazil" in a journal article title. And it does. And the reader who couldn't find articles on "Hostages" in *Psychological Abstracts* simply had to look up that precise word in the *SSCI* to find over a score of hits.

Key word searches thus frequently allow much more precise retrieval than subject heading searches; and as an alternative to the latter they involve much less hit-or-miss searching than does the technique of browsing or using a classification scheme. With a key word search you can zero in very quickly to the exact words you are looking for.

There is a trade-off involved, however. The price you pay for such precise access is the loss of synonym control—that is, with key word indexes you *do* have to think up all of the variant ways in which a subject can be expressed. If, for example, you look up only the words "capital" and "punishment", you will miss all the citations that use the terms "death penalty" or "execution" or "death row". And there will be *no cross-references* to lead you from one term to the other. Similarly you must be careful to look up variant singular, plural and possessive forms of the same word (*e.g.*, "child", "child's", "children", "children's"). Such problems are solved for you in subject heading indexes—that is the peculiar strength of controlled vocabularies. Their weakness is that they often lack precise enough terms, or terms that are up-to-date; but here the key word sources have their peculiar strength. The advantages and disadvantages of the two types of indexes are thus neatly complementary.

All researchers should at least be aware of the three basic ISI indexes, for collectively they provide access to all subject areas through a key word approach. These three, however, are by no means the only sources offering key word access to knowledge records.

What is more important than remembering a list of specific titles, however, is that you remember the *technique* of key word searching with its advantages and disadvantages, as an alternative to subject heading searches. And—just as with subject heading indexes—each of these key word sources covers many subjects beyond whatever area of concentration may be mentioned in its title (*e.g.*, "Women" and 'Computers" can be found in *all* of them). No matter what your subject, in other words, *several* key word indexes will cover it. You can always assume that this method of searching is available for pursuing an inquiry.

A reference librarian often finds that the first question to ask is whether or not a good subject heading exists that corresponds to a researcher's need; if there is one, then a whole class of sources can be brought to bear on the problem. But if there isn't, then we can readily shift gears and use another approach that involves a distinctly different class of sources: key word indexes. Nor is this approach confined to journal indexes.

The key word search capability is involved in many alternatives:

- Dictionaries.
- Encyclopaedias (especially those with a separate index volume).
- Card catalogue (*i.e.*, by looking for the first word of a book's title as a key word).
- Index pages at the ends of monographs.
- Browsing through texts of books.
- Manual key word indexes such as those described above.

- Computer searches.
- *The Encyclopaedia of Associations* (key word index).
- Talking to people.

All these methods and sources allow you to get around the problem of not finding a good subject heading for what you want.

The three basic ISI indexes should be kept in mind especially by scholars who wish to pursue cross-disciplinary inquiries. Each of them covers a vast range of subjects and so brings to bear on any inquiry a huge range of journals from many disciplines.

Collectively, the three ISI indexes summon the cross-disciplinary resources of approximately 6000 journals in all fields for use on any subject that may interest you.

REFERENCES

1. *How to Use Shepard's Citations* (Shepard's/McGraw-Hill, 1980).
2. Eugene Garfield, *Citation Indexing: Its Theory and Application in Science, Technology and Humanities* (John Wiley & Sons, 1979)."

2

Automated Acquisition System

> "The lover of books is a minor, searching for gold all his life long. He finds nuggets, his heart leaps in his breast; he cannot believe in his good fortune.
>
> Traversing a slow page, to come upon a lode of the pure shining metal is to exult inwardly for greedy hours. It belongs to no one else; it is not interchangeable.
>
> —*Kathleen Norris.*

As we have already intended in the preceding chapter, our aim is to elucidate various library systems in digital age, here we come to computer-based acquisition system in modern libraries.

We shall now come a case study of an operational computer-based acquisitions system that applied the major principles and aspects of designing a system as outlined in the previous chapter. This case study is intended to illustrate the characteristics of the computer system used as well as the input/output media involved in satisfying the system's requirements.

Characteristics of the Computer System

The capabilities and limitations of computer system available to the library must be known prior to deigning the computer-based library system. In the case of the described acquisitions system the equipment available to the library was in International Business Machine System 360/50 computer installation consisting of the following devices listed with their IBM type number and related capabilities.

1. First there was a 2050 central processing unit (CPU) with type 1052 typewriter and console that could handle compilation and execution of programmes together. CPU core storage is 131,172 bytes (characters)., Two 16-digit decimals may be multiplied together in 37.25 microsecond. This speed of data handling is illustrated by the fact that 18 three-line bibliographic records (call number, author, and title) plus a page heading may be formatted for printing in less than 1 second including an edit (Verification) of the call number and allowance for spaces between entries.
2. There were two 1403 line printers for printed output. Each printer is rated at 600 lines per minute with 132 characters per line using a printing chain with the Standard Character Set of 48 graphics (26 upper case alpha, 10 numeric, and 12 assorted special characters). Using the Full Character Set (Text Printing) chain, which includes upper and lower case letters, numerals, and many more special characters than the Standard Set, printing speed is reduced by more than 50 per cent to about 250 lines per minute.
3. A 2540 card reader punch was available for reading punched-card input and punching output data. This machine reads 1000 cards per minute and punches 300 cards per minute.

4. There were four 2311 disk drives that house "compilers" and the various monitor systems." Compilers are programmes that translate instructions in specific programmes into the language that the machine can use. Monitor systems coordinate and direct the computer system's capabilities for maximum effectiveness in processing user programmes. There are 7.25 million characters of random (direct) access storage available from each disk drive and it may be read at 56,000 characters per second. Direct access is essential to such operations as sorting or putting a file in some desired order.. For example, 3000 variable-length records can be alphabetized in less than 3 minutes including the time it takes for the input and output magnetic tapes to be rewound.
5. Five 2400 model 1 magnetic tape drives for general input/output (I/O) operations were avai-lable. There are 23 million characters of sequential storage available per tape drive deliverable at 30,000 characters per second. The tapes are useful or files that will be used but not rearranged in processing.
6. A 2671 paper-tape reader was provided. With the feed and take-up spools, paper tape is read at 1000 characters (about three book orders) per second. The spooling accessory allows tapes to be read in proper data sequence without respect to how the paper tape is wound.
7. A 2361 bulk core storage provided over one million bytes of core storage supplementing the storage capacity available in the central processing unit.
8. A 2841 control unit for the disk 2311 drives and a

2821 control unit for the 1403 printers and the 2540 reader were available to synchronize the I/O devices with the CPU so that the programme processing would continue during the I/O operations. Being mechanical, these operations are considerably slower than the electronic operations of the CPU.

9. Peripheral utility type equipment was also available including the 129 keypunch, the burster for breaking apart paper printout, the decollator for pulling out carbon paper and separating multiple copies of a printout, the punched-card duplicating machine, and the punched-card sorter.

Systems Chart

When the decision to purchase a book was made, the analyst could see the effect this would have on the acquisition system as well as others. He applied the principle of economy of recording information only once and began the design that could satisfy this principle. He also kept in mind five major internal requirements that the new acquisitions system had to satisfy: a current on-order file, a claiming procedure, a notification to requestor, various fiscal reports, and operating statistics. In order to satisfy the system need for records in two forms, eye legible and machine readable, an input device was needed to create the records in these formats. The key punch, although it produces punched cards that are eye legible and machine readable, was unacceptable because it could not prepare the needed multiple-copy order sets.

On the other hand the paper type that serves as input to the computer. The advantage of the tape typewriter over the key punch in this ordering application appear to be: (i) the production of a conventional, typed record that facilitates the revision and making of corrections, and (ii) the familiarity of the typewriter as a tool to all library clerical personnel.

The tape typewriter used in this application is controlled by a master tape that performs the following functions:

1. Positions the order form and controls the horizontal and vertical positioning of data.
2. Maintains control over format of data to be entered. For example, if in a certain area it is required that four characters of information be inserted into the record and if the operator only centers three characters of information, the machine will stop and not continue until the field has been filled.
3. The control tape automatically inserts into the input tape the necessary control characters to identify the beginning and end of each variable-length field.

Satisfaction of the requirements resulted first in a multipart book order form that was designed to 'fulfill the existing requirements as well as to provide the necessary input for computer processing. The function of typing the book-order set and the disposition of the output in terms of external and internal requirements.

Parts one, two, and three of the multipart form may be considered as satisfying external requirements; copy 1 to be used for the vendor's records; copy 2 to go to the vendor for return with the book or for use as a report on the book's availability; and copy 3 to be used for ordering Library of Congress catalogue cards and on return, as notification to the individual requestor of the book's availability. Part 4 is filed in the interim in-process file until the order appears on the weekly computer-produced in-process list.

The paper tape provides the input for various other requirements satisfied by computer-produced reports.

1. *Current On-order File.* Under manual procedures continuous control and updating of such a file is nearly impossible. However, it is possible to update the file keep it current with the computer-based system. Further, the computer-produced on-order file reduces the manual filing operation to the maintenance of a weekly interim in-process file. The computer-produced in-process list provides a biweekly cumulated list of orders including any changes made after the original typing of the order.

2. Because the conditions under which a claim was initiated had to be specified in detail, this requirement cold be well satisfied by a computer-based record.

3. *Fiscal Reports.* In order to keep an accurate and current account of the encumbrances and expenditures of the acquisitions, system, a variety of fiscal reports were required. As the record-keeping function increased in volume and complexity the more amenable it became to computer-based manipulation. One of the fiscal reports includes statements of funds added, withdrawn, expenditures year to date, encumbered funds, and previous and current balances for each account.

4. *Operating Statistics.* As the volume of book orders increased the task of keeping statistics obviously became more complex. The requirement of maintaining a variety of routine statistical reports and producing special reports as needed was suited to a computer control.

Computer Processing Storage and Output Media

It was established that the initial computer input was

to be the punched-paper tape produced by the tape typewriter and that the records were then to be stored on magnetic tape for processing by the computer. The design of the machine-readable record and the system for processing it had to be developed within the framework of these two parameters, paper tape for input and magnetic tape for processing and storage.

In designing the machine record and specifying the processing the first step was translation of the record from the punched-paper tape into the magnetic-tape code, which is a character-by-character translation. Here advantage was taken of the computer's abilities to structure in a predetermined format, a magnetic-tape record that makes provision for all essential data elements whether or not they are present in the record being translated. It the translated magnetic-tape record was to be readily updated throughout, if each new record could contain any or all of the allowable data elements, and if records could be entered in random order, additional parameters had to be considered to further develop the system.

Consequently, two major programmes were developed: the translation programme, including formatting and editing of the record, and a general processing programme. The two programmes had to be separated by another programme because of two other seemingly incompatible requirements: that records be readily updated and that they bee accepted in random order. To update a record it first had to be found in the file. Finding it required that it be uniquely identifiable and implied, with sequential access storage (magnetic tape), that the records were in specified order. Thus each record had to have a code (handle) by which it could be located in the computer file.

After a record was found, the specific part of it that was to be updated had to be identifiable and accessible within the record itself. Computer records come in two basic formats: fixed length and variable length. Using the former of satisfy the updating requirement was the logical choice since most of the records would contain predictable elements of data; for example, author, title and publisher.

A size limit was set that was large enough to accommodate the longest expected variable of each element. Each element then had its own field (fixed) in the same place in every record regardless of whether the field contained valid data for merely blanks supplied during translation. From a programming standpoint, in this application, fixed-length fields and records were considered much more convenient to work with than variable-length fields and records.

Remarkably, at this stage in the design of the machine record and the processing system the following points were decided upon:

1. Each record to have a unique number and was to contain fixed-length data fields.
2. A computer translation programme that would accept paper-tape input developed to: (i) translate the punched code into computer code, (ii) edit the translated data for validity, and (iii) format the data onto a magnetic tape for further processing.
3. A sort programme to arrange the records by their unique numbers.
4. A processing programme to update the records.
5. Additional programmes to produce from the update master file output needed to satisfy the

overall requirements of the system; for example, a printed in-process list and a current accession list.

Further, to explain more fully the computer translation programme (item 2), editing the data elements was possible with the parameters established for valid data in any given field. If a price field, for example was defined as one containing only digits or the letters GIFT, then a gift book coded as FREE in that field would be considered an error by the edit feature of the programme. Such invalid data were to be printed out in an error listing for correcting the input.

Formatting Records

The formatting of the records was done by the programmer after the data elements had been established for the acquisitions system. It was here that the programmer played an important role. Balancing the needs of the system against the capabilities of the computer, he developed a tape format that would take maximum advantage of the machine's size, speed, and logic features to meet the requirements of the system.

In fact, all but three of the fields in the figure are supplied directly by the paper-tape input. Content in the three fields named CONNO (control number), CLAIMS, and STATUS, each indicated by arrows, is supplied entirely under computer programme control as a product of data processing but there is a difference between the data in CLAIMS and that in either CONNO or STATUS. The data in CLAIMS is *informative;* that is, if the record were printed out, the characters in the field would supply information directly to the reader without need of translation. It should be remembered that one of the original demands made of the record was that it contain all the codes or *indicators* enabling it to be processed. CONNO and STATUS are examples of indicator fields. One feature of the system/360 computer that makes it a powerful data processing tool is its ability to access, test, and manipulate individual *bits* within a *byte*. A byte is composed of eight bits and represents one alphabetic or special character, two decimal digits or right binary bits of information. A byte for the letter A, for example, has the bits arranged thus: 1100000. By assigning each bit position a 1 or a 0 (on, off), eight separate conditions or any combination thereof may be carried in one byte. The two fields STATUS and CONNO are each two-byte-long "message centers" with a combined potential for identifying 32 separate conditions. The data in STATUS and CONNO, then, are indicative rather than informative. If a particular record were printed out, its bit patterns, in STATUS and CONNO might or might not have a graphic representation on the printout and even if they did, the graphic would mean nothing in itself until it could be reduced to its own bit pattern and then interpreted. The combined four bytes of CONNO and STATUS may be used to indicate internally a record's condition and stage of processing throughout the time it is under programme control. Most conditions are best shown by the use of the CONNO and STATUS bit pattern "flags" rather than by relying on the presence or absence of information within the record. The presence of price data, for example, does not show that an item has been paid for, but a bit that can be set only when the invoice is cleared and paid shows the item as paid.

Sorting and Utility Programmes and Macro Instructions

It ispertinent to note that the process of sorting is

accomplished by utility programmes. These programmes usually are supplied by the computer manufacturer. They are very general and flexible with broad computer applications such as sorting a file, merging files, and punching, cards. There are usually few limitations on the use of such programmes and normally all the user needs to do is to describe the characteristics of his file and individual record to a particular utility programme.

In using a utility programme for a sorting operation the input and output devices are designated first, the size of the file is given, then the individual record is specified as to its length, the position and length of the fields to be sorted (given in the order in which they are to be printed out—such as by order number, author, and title); and the sequence of the sort whether in ascending or descending order. Related to the utility programmes are the macro instructions. A definition of macro, "of or involving large quantities," implies its use.

In computer terminology a macro is an instruction having the capability of generating more than one machine-language instruction and is incorporated under a coded name into the monitor system of the particular machine. Thereafter when the macro's code name command is given, the monitor system expands it into the predefined set of instructions.

Some commonly used macros are open, close, read, write, get, put, print, and punch. Generally in an actual instruction these macros would be followed by one or more file names showing what device or file the specified command is to act on. The macro facility in general provides convenient shortcuts for the programmer and wherever necessary he can write his own macros.

If, for example, under certain conditions. *A* were to be replaced by *a* many times in several different programmes, the programmer could elect to write a macro called "replace" which would contain all the instructions necessary to replace *A* with *a*.

The sort procedure operates with a nondestructive readout. At the conclusion of a sort there is not just a single file in a different order from that with which the sort began but two files. The original file is not erased or in any way destroyed n the process of being sorted. In the acquisitions system s utility sort is used prior to the update programme to produce a file sorted first by order number and then within the order number by the transaction codes to bring each record and its associated updating information together in a predetermined order for processing by the update programme.

As previously stated the system was to accept updating information in random order but a sort was necessary between the translation and update programmes because the records on both the master and transactions files are in sequential order to expedite matching of update data with the proper master record.

Update and Update Programme

Infact, the term "update" is very general and may be roughly equated to the expression "file maintenance." In a strict interpretation this involves modifying a master file with current information according to a specified procedure that could include an exchange of characters for blanks or if the master record is being corrected, an exchange of valid characters for invalid ones.

Using presorted input the steps of the file maintenance

programme are to match each transaction to the proper master record, identify the type of transaction (price or date received) an enter new data or corrected data. The designation "update programme" was given the file maintenance procedure of updating combined with other procedures. While the primary achievement of the update programme is a current on-order file, such features as bit testing and manipulation and speed of processing make it practical to satisfy other system requirements concurrently.

Output is produced as a by-product of processing each record including such useful procedures as statists on books ordered and received, reports on the amounts encumbered and spent from various funds, list of errors in input data, and a file of items for which processing has been completed.

New Trends in Acquisitions System

From the design of the acquisitions system under discussion a core of programmed processing emerged that included facets of the operations in the acquisitions subsystems. In a computer-based system the core of programme processing will often cut across the boundaries of subsystem as they existed before the new system was initiated. In this acquisitions system the various operations and functions of the manually maintained subsystems had to be realigned with the revised subsystems for the newly designed system to be effective. As a case in point we can consider the four acquisitions subsystem of preorder searching, ordering, accounting and reporting, and receiving and checking. The changes within the redesigned system are shown as follows:

Before	*After*
Preorder searching	Unchanged
Ordering	Ordering, I/O preparation and processing
Accounting and reporting	Data processing
Receiving and checking	Receiving, I/O preparation and processing

At east one major operation of ordering, the maintenance of an in-process file, has been taken over by the new subsystem data processing. Similarly the operation of maintaining account balances, previously maintained by accounting and reporting is now absorbed by data processing. The original requirements of the system are still being satisfied and further the new system has the potential of satisfying increases in these requirements.

Salient Features of Integrated Systems Design

In planning the design of the acquisition system that we have been discussing, the total-systems approach was used in considering the placing of the routine and data processing operations of the system under machine control. As part of the design of the computer-based acquisitions system it was decided that punched cards for the circulation system should be produced from the magnetic-tape acquisitions record file after it has been updated with call numbers.

The programme produced a master machine-readable circulation card for a currently processed book. This card, which lists the accession number, the author or title, and the call number, was inserted into the book. This procedure was the first phase in implementing the computer-based circulation system while still operating under manual conditions.

Because, new books are expected to circulate more than the old and because most new and circulating materials are equipped with punched cards, the automated circulation system should be fully operational at the time of installation. Another output produced after the machine-readable acquisitions record has been updated with call numbers is the accessions list. It is arranged by call number and provides the author and title of each book. This bimonthly listing is distributed by the reference librarians as a current awareness service to users. It is different from the in-process list in that the accessions list is shelf list of newly cataloged books. It is intended to a allow persons interested in a given subject to scan a pertinent block of call numbers and be aware of new library acquisitions that may related to his field of interest. As a requirement of the machine-readable acquisitions file it was decided that the file should be a historical (retrospective) record primarily for the possible use of these records as the means to find and "lift" full machine-readable cataloging data from MARC tapes or from some other library's cataloging data bank. This is seen as a way to save time and effort when the decision is made to convert existing cataloging records to machine-readable form.

It is obvious from the preceding discussion that that Acquisition system in libraries has undergone sea changes than the traditional system. With the introduction of new electronic devices we may aspire for significant imporvements in future libraries.

3

Automated Collection Management Systems

> "One cool judgement is worth a hasty councils. The ghing to do is to supply light and not heat."
>
> —*Woodrwo Wilson*

In the preceding chapter we have highlighted automate/ computer-based acquisition system in modern libraries. Now we will describe computer-based collection system.

As is widely experienced, automated systems can provide data on the use of library collections that are more complete than those available in the preautomation era. Consequently, collection development policies and collection management in general, should now be better than they were in the past. "Better" here implies decisions that are more effective or more cost–effective: buying more of the things that patrons really need, buying fewer that will never be used or used only rarely, buying more items whose cost–per–use will be low. Various aspects of the use of automated systems in collection management have been dealt with in the literature. Perhaps the most complete overview is that of Nutter (1987).

As Nutter (1987) points out, the online catalog, representing what the library now owns, can be used to produce a detailed analysis of the present collection. Tabulations can be produced for such variables as language, country of publication, data of publication, subject and publication type and useful correlations can also be made–for example, between subject and language or subject and data of publication. Simple but detailed analyses of this type might in themselves suggest strengths and weaknesses in the collection and the data can be used to monitor changes over time. In an academic setting, the analyses of holdings can be compared with "profiles" of the various academic departments or faculties, where these profiles are defined by numbers from the scheme of classification used to organize the collection.

Here, a good example of the analysis of the holdings of academic libraries can be found in the work of Kountz (1991), who compared holdings data with data on student course enrollment to measure the extent to which collections match "constituency interests."

Nutter (1987) suggests that one approach to the evaluation of a collection is to compare it with external databases to identify strengths, weaknesses, items that should probably be acquired, and so on. This seems particularly appropriate to the special library situation. For example, a medical library might compare its monograph acquisitions over, say, the last five years with the acquisitions of the National Library of Medicine (NLM) in the same time period, as represented in NLM's monographic database. Comparisons could be made on the basis of class numbers, where the local library makes use of NLM's classification, or subject headings.

The ratio of local library acquisitions to NLM acquisitions in various subject areas could be taken as an indicator of areas in which the local library appears strong and areas in which it appears weak. Another type of holdings/database comparison involves the use of databases searched online on behalf of library users. The bibliographic references actually retrieved in such searches presumably reflect the interests of library users, or at least those who make use of the database searching service.

By downloading the references retrieved by all searches performed during a particular period of time, a useful database can be created. Analyses can then be performed on the resulting data. Most obviously, one can produce a list of journals ranked by the number of times they have been retrieved and this may reveal certain titles that should perhaps be added to the collection because they seem to match current community interests rather closely. Again, this type of analysis is likely to be more valuable in the special library than in the general library.

Circulation Analysis

Although it has always been possible to perform analyses of circulation records to study use of the collection, at least on a sampling basis, studies of this kind are greatly facilitated when circulation is automated. Records representing all circulations, rather than a sample, can be manipulated by computer program to produce data on subject distribution of the circulation, to identify the most heavily used titles and (if the data are collected for a sufficiently long period) to measure rate of obsolescence. The most obvious application of circulation data is to produce analyses of use of the collection by subject according to the various subdivisions of the classification scheme in use in the library. Jain (1965–1969) pointed out that librarians should be less concerned with establishing the absolute use of portions of a collection than with determining "relative" use. What this really means is that one should use circulation data to reveal differences between actual and "expected" behavior.

Suppose, for example, that books on physics make up 12% of a particular collection. Probability alone suggests that physics books should account for 12% of the circulation. If they do, that portion of the collection is behaving exactly as expected. On the other hand, if physics books account for only 8% of the circulation, one can say that the class is "underused" (used less than expected) whereas it would be "overused" if it accounts for, say, 15% of all circulation. An overused class is one in which items are used more than expected (in a probabilistic sense) relative to the proportion of the collection occupied by that class.

An underused class is one in which items are used less than expected relative to the proportion of the collection occupied by that class. If data on the library's holdings in various classes are built into an automated circulation system, printouts or displays can be generated to show for each class what proportion of the collection it occupies and what proportion of the circulation it accounts for. The table shows that circulation in 620 and 640 is close to what is expected, while classes 610 and 650 are heavily overused and 630 is heavily underused. An automated circulation system could be used to generate such data in a more useful format; e.g., identify those classes that deviate most from the expected behavior–those most overused and those most underused.

Notably, the assumption is that the most deviant classes are those that need most attention. The circulation data merely highlight the deviant classes; they do not tell the librarian how to deal with them. One could argue that both overused and underused classes may fail to meet user needs. If a class is heavily overused, the implication is that the library lacks the strength in this area to meet the present volume and variety of demands. The more overused a class, the lower the probability that any particular book will be on the shelf when looked for by a user. Moreover, the more overused the class, the less valuable it will be to the browser because of the phenomenon of "shelf bias." Shelfbias refers to the fact that, all other things being equal, the shelves of a library will tend to display books that nobody wants to borrow.

The phenomenon was identified explicitly by Buckland (1972) and Buckland and Hindle (1969), who referred to it as "collection bias." "Shelfbias" seems more descriptive of what is actually taking place. Buckland (1975) expresses the bias in terms of the proportion of the material absent from the shelves at a particular time. Thus, if 80 books out of 240 were absent, the bias would be 33%. A heavily underused class may be just as disturbing as one heavily overused. The class appears not to be of much interest to the community. This may reflect changing interests over time. On-the other hand, it may indicate that the selection of books is just not a good one. Perhaps the library is buying the wrong books (e.g., too technical or too the - oretical) or that it owns too many books that are out–of–date and should be discarded. It is possible that use of the class would increase substantially if it were thoroughly weeded and more attractive, up-to-date items added. Circulation data can bring "problem" classes to the librarians's attention. It is then the librarian's task to look more closely at such classes to decide why they are behaving as they are and what corrective action appears to be necessary.

It is significant to note that degree of discrepancy between holdings and circulation can be expressed in several ways. The simplest, perhaps, is the "circulation/inventory ratio" (C/I) used by Wenger et al. (1979), which is nothing more than the number of circulations occurring in a class during a particular period of time divided by the number of items in that class. Thus, a class with seven items and twenty circulations receives a C/I ratio of 2.9 (20/7), i.e., approximately 2.9 uses per item per x period of time (usually a year). Dowlin and Magrath (1983) also use this but refer to it as "inventory use ratio." The Public Library Association (PLA), in its output measures for public libraries (Van House et al., 1987), uses the term "turnover rate" for the same measure (i.e., uses per item per year). Following the recommendations of the PLA and of various state library agencies, many public libraries in the United States collect turnover data, although few seem to make intelligent use of them. In fact, the turnover rate for a complete collection is of very little interest (except, perhaps, in comparing the performance of similar libraries).

What is of interest is the turnover rate for various parts of the collection. The turnover rate for adult nonfiction as a whole (1.11) masks the fact that the turnover ranges from a low of .51 (about one half of a use per book per year) for class 800 to 1.84 for class 400. The table shows how turnover rate correlates well with relative use.

For example, class 400 has high relative use (circulation is almost twice what probability suggests it should be) and the highest turnover and class 800, with the lowest turnover rate, is used at exactly half the level expected (10% of the collection and 5% of the use).

Day and Revill (1995) discuss a variant on turnover rate in which recent acquisitions only are related to circulation. While this makes sense, it would make even more sense to compare circulation with both total holdings and recent acquisitions.

Nimmer (1980) has used the measure "intensity of circulation" —number of circulations per 100 titles held. Bonn (1974) proposed a simple "use factor" (renamed as "degree of use" by Gillentine et al., 1981), which is the proportion (or percentage) of the circulation accounted for by a class divided by the proportion of the collection occupied by that class.

With this type of ratio, as used by Jenks (1976), the higher the figure the greater the overuse. For example, a class accounting for 3.49% of the collection and 4.79% of the circulation receives a score of 137.25 while one that accounts for .36% of the collection but only .16% of the circulation gets a score of 44.44. Metz (1983) refers to this measure as the "proportional use statistic" and Aguilar (1986) as "percentage of expected use." Aguilar derived his use of this measure from Mills (1982). Trochim et al. (1980) use the *difference* between holdings percentage and collection percentage for each class as an indicator of overuse or underuse.

Mills (1982) is critical of this: a difference of 0.2 would apply equally to a subject occupying 0.5% of the collection and getting 0.7% of the use as it would to one occupying 2.5% of the collection and getting 2.7% of use, yet the proportional discrepancy between holdings and use is very much greater for the smaller class.

Mostyn (1974) uses the term "supply–demand equality" in referring to the relative use relationship; an overused class is one in which demand exceeds supply and vice versa for an underused class. Mills (1982) has applied the relative use principle to the problems of collection development in a film library. In a typical film library, films have to be "booked" (i.e., reserved) in advance, so it has an advantage over most other types of library in that failure rates (i.e., "denials" –cases when particular films or films of a certain type are not available to the requester) are easy to identify and record. Mills makes use of this failure rate, as well as a measure of relative use, to make decisions relating to future acquisitions.

The percentage of holdings related to the percentage of bookings gives a percentage of expected use. Thus, art films account for 1% of holdings and 0.88% of bookings, so the percentage of expected use is 88. The denial to bookings ratio brings in further data. A high D/B ratio means that films in this category are unlikely to be available when needed by a user. The worst case us "stories–holidays and seasons," where 74% of the requests for films have to be denied (D/B ratio = 0.74). On the basis of relative use data (percentage of expected use), the difference between percentage of bookings and percentage of holdings and D/B ratio, Mills is able to make recommendations relating to future acquisitions: some classes need to be strengthened by further purchases, which might be further copies of things already owned ("add prints"), some need to be weeded and some should be strengthened and weeded.

Notably, Britten (1990) uses the "80/20" rule as the basis of a study of circulation in an academic library. He found that, while the rule seemed to apply to the complete collection, substantial differences among the LC classes could be observed. For one subclass, 40% of the items are needed to account for 80% of the circulations. At the other extreme is a class in which only 1.5% of the items account for 80% of the use. He advocates that the classes that deviate most from the 80/20 distribution in a positive way (a higher proportion needed to account for 80% of the use) should be "rewarded" in future collection development and budget allocation. Clearly, this type of comparison of the performance of various categories of books is merely another variant of relative use or the turnover rate.

Lee and Lockway (1991) also use percentage of expected use to indicate the most deviant classes in the collection, in this case in an academic library. At one extreme, class HV5001, which accounts for 0.0809% of the collection, gets 0.559^{8}% of the use, a use factor (UF) of 6.92 or a PEU (percentage of expected use) of 692. In contrast, class LH earns a UF of only 0.03 and a PEU of 3.

In fact, there are other ways of expressing overuse and underuse of portions of the collection. One is the proportion of items on loan (and, conversely, the proportion that should be on the shelf) at a particular time. A class in which many of the items are in use is a healthy class whereas one from which few items are borrowed is not—little interest exists in this subject in the community, the library is not buying the right books, or the class contains too much that is obsolete. On the other hand, it is not good to have a class in which most books are always absent from the shelves; this would indicate considerable shelf bias and the probability that a user would find particular item on the shelf when needed must be very low.

Extremely active classes of this kind need strengthening, at least through the purchase of further copies of the most used items. The monitoring of collection use by proportions of classes absent from the shelves is not dependent on automation and, in fact, predated automated systems (see, for example, McClellan, 1956, 1978).

Nevertheless, such monitoring is much easier when

data can be drawn from an automated circulation system. Note the very wide differences between heavily used classes, in which more than 20% of the items are on loan and little used classes, in which less than 5% are in use. In performing analyses of this kind, items that cannot be borrowed (i.e., reference only) should obviously be excluded. It is also possible to use the circulation system to "flag" items that are now used so heavily that additional copies should be purchased or some other steps taken to improve their availability.

Special Databases

It is further worth mentioning that analyses of circulation patterns of the type discussed in the preceding section are based on data that can be drawn from an existing database–that recording which items are borrowed, when and by whom. But it is also possible to build other databases that can be useful in making decisions relating to collection development and management. One such database would record in–house use of the collection. In the past, it has been notoriously difficult to get good data on in–library use (Rubin, 1986; Lancaster, 1993a).

Today, however, portable data collection devices can be used to scan bar codes or OCR labels on books left on tables or in carrels in the library before they are returned to the shelves. This procedure is likely to underestimate the total volume of inhouse use, perhaps rather considerably, because not all uses will involve carrying items to seats in the library and many items may be returned to shelves by users (Lancaster, 1993a).

Nevertheless, it should depict the pattern of inhouse use fairly accurately: if the data show that X items are used five times more than Y items, this probably does reflect the relative use of these two sets, even though both counts may be underestimates. Rapidly escalating costs, coupled with budgets diminishing in purchasing power, have forced many libraries to discontinue subscriptions to some periodicals or other serials. To aid decisions on which serials to discontinue, it may be valuable to build a database of information on the serials that the library now receives. Such a database has been described by Hansen (1986). The most difficult data to collect, of course, are those on recorded use. If these can not be collected through use of scanning devices, as mentioned earlier, they can be obtained in various ways on a sampling basis, as described by Lancaster (1993a).

Although Hansen records binding cost, she does not calculate a total ownership cost, based on estimates of storage and handling costs as well as subscription and binding costs. The data she does record would allow an estimate to be made of cost per use (see Chrzastowski, 1991, for example) for each serial based on subscription cost and binding cost, but use related to an estimate of total ownership cost would be more accurate. Of course, the construction of a database of this kind and its updating and maintenance, require an investment on the part of the library.

Hansen suggests that the investment is justifiable because the database makes readily available the information needed to make deselection decisions and has value in other applications–e.g., to generate printouts of serials relevant to particular academic departments and to provide data useful to binding operations. Although the database described by Hansen is designed for use in academia, it could obviously be modified for use by other types of libraries. All of the elements other than department–

relatedness are equally relevant to other libraries and alternative data could be substituted as appropriate.

For another type of database can be built to record interlibrary loan transactions as described, for example, by Wessling (1989) and Chang (1990). Interlibrary loans initiated online, by staff members or library users, can be recorded automatically and others added manually. A database of this kind may be useful in a number of different ways.

For example, it could be used to:

1. Identify requests made by particular constituencies (e.g., academic departments).
2. Identify monographs or journals requested more than X times.
3. Identify subject areas in which many requests are made.
4. Provide data that can be compared with other data, such as those relating to circulation and acquisitions patterns.

Data Comparisons

Decisions relating to the development and management of collections will be most firmly based when they take into account more than circulation data alone–hence the value of the specially constructed databases discussed in the previous section.

Data on circulation, in–house use, interlibrary loan and current acquisition patterns can all be useful. For example, one needs to know, for any particular subject area, what the level of current purchasing is and whether use of the class is increasing or decreasing over time. Consider the following hypothetical data that could be gene-rated from a management information system within a library:

> Class y is very much underused and use continues to decline. This would appear to be a class in which interest is waning and it seems hard to justify the fact that 3.5% of all acquisitions fall in an area that accounts for only 0.2% of current circulation. Similar data for other classes could lead to quite different conclusions.

For example, if a class is under-used and on the decline but percentage of current acquisitions is well below percentage of collection, the situation seems to have corrected itself and no further action is called for. The librarian should look at fine circulation data rather than coarse to avoid jumping to the wrong conclusions. The fact that Dewey class 600 is overused does not necessarily mean that the entire class is overused; it may be that only the cookbooks are overused and all other subdivisions are actually underused.

Likewise, overuse of Library of Congress class QA may suggest the need for strengthening of the entire mathematics collection when, in fact, it is only the computer science books that are affecting the results. Of course, automated circulation systems can yield data that are finer than gross use patterns; use of small subclasses or even individual titles can be examined. One example of this type of analysis can be found in Britten and Webster (1992), who analyzed MARC records for titles heavily used within an academic library in an attempt to identify common characteristics that might predict use of future additions to the collection.

Common elements examined were subject heading, author, language and imprint date. Byrd et al. (1982) have described a method for determining strengths and weaknesses in a collection based on the difference in proportions between the subject breakdown of a library's acquisitions and the subject breakdown of the interlibrary loan requests it generates. The theory is that the classes needing greatest attention are those in which the greatest difference exists between volume of materials borrowed and volume of materials purchased.

Payne and Willers (1989) have shown how circulation data can be related to acquisitions data to measure success in materials selection (expressed, for example, by the proportion of items purchased in subject X that have circulation within period Y). Success may also be related to source of selection–e.g., faculty versus librarian selection in the case of some academic libraries. Aguilar (1984) performed a monumental study of the relationship between internal circulation and interlibrary loan requests based on about 86,000 interlibrary loan (ILL) transactions and almost two million circulation records from eighteen Illinois libraries.

He found support for his hypothesis that a class that is overused (as defined earlier) in a library will be a class in which the library will borrow many items, whereas underused classes tend not to generate large numbers of ILL requests. This support the assumption that it is overused classes rather than underused classes that are most in need of strengthening.

Nutter (1987) recommends that academic libraries should study interrelations among databases representing holdings, circulation, and patron characteristics. Patron files can be coded by department/discipline to allow comparisons of usage and to study what types of materials are used each department. In the case of academic and special libraries, the patron file could actually identify all potential users, allowing the librarian to derive a user/nonuser ratio for the community as a whole and possibly for each department. Another source of information of potential value in collection development is the online catalog and its actual use by library patrons.

Possibly useful information can be obtained from several report generation features existing within commercially available system. For example, the INNOPAC system will identify the names of authors most used within a particular time period and the subject terms introduced by users that do not retrieve any items. While the latter will often be symptomatic of errors in user terminology, or search logic, they may occa-sionally indicate gaps in subject coverage in the collection. In theory, interactions between library users and the catalog could be monitored to identify (1) books sought that are not in the collection and (2) books sought and found to be in the collection but not immediately available on the shelves (which could be used to produce an estimate of availability rate).

However, this presupposes that users must employ some unambiguous identifier for a book rather than a truncation algorithm that is equivocal.

While all of the analyses discussed so far can based on data obtainable from library catalogs, circulation systems, acquisitions systems or other databases, this will usually require the writing of special programs for extraction and manipulation since the commercially available systems are not likely to offer the capabilities sought as a standard feature. Features that are present in many existing systems include: (1) ability to record circulation by type of patron, (2) ability to identify the most heavily used classes, (3) ability to identify books for which many "holds" are placed and (4) ability to identify books not borrowed within a particular period of time (Hawks, 1988). Unfortunately, while automated systems can be used to generate better data for collection management than librarians have had before, the advantage is more theoretical than actual. Not only do commercially produced systems fail to provide convenient access to the most useful data but many librarians seem unconvinced of the value of the data (Carrigan, 1996).

Availability of Materials

The factors that affect the availability of books owned by a library have been thoroughly discussed by Buckland (1975). The most important are level of demand (popularity), number of copies and length of loan period. It is obvious that the more popular a particular book the less likely it is to be on the shelf at any particular time. 'Popularity" is not a nebulous measure in this case, but a very practical one. As mentioned earlier, it can be expressed in terms of a last circulation date.

That is, one could say that 10% of the collection circulated at least once in the last month, 25% circulated at least once in the last six months and so on. It seems equally obvious that buying additional copies will improve availability. But two copies are not twice as good as one copy–sometimes both are on the shelf, sometimes one, sometimes neither–and the addition of further copies may make only a marginal difference to availability. The effect of adding an additional copy varies with the popularity of the item: if a particular book is never used it will always be available and adding a second copy does not change the situation. If a book is off the shelf for one half of the year, one can say its availability rate is 0.5. Adding a second copy will improve availability but will not double it (Leimkuhler, 1966).

Buckland (1975) presents data to show the effect of varying numbers of duplicate copies on the availability of books at different levels of popularity. Less obvious, perhaps, are the effects on availability of the length of the loan period. Suppose that every user of a library returns a book on or near the day on which it is due to be returned.

There is, in fact, a strong tendency for this to occur, as reported by Newhouse and Alexander (1972), Buckland (1975), and Goehlert (1979). Then, reducing the length of the loan period from four weeks greatly increases the probability that any book will be available on the shelf when looked for by a user. In fact, cutting the length of the period in half has roughly the same effect on availability as buying a second copy. The librarian can improve the accessibility of books by buying more copies of popular items, reducing the length of the loan period, or both. In fact, if one wished, it would be possible to identify a desired "satisfaction level" (e.g., 0.8–a user will find a desired item to be on the shelf in eight cases out of ten) and take steps to ensure that this level would apply to every book in the library. Suppose one divided the collection into five levels of popularity on the basis of most recent circulation date.

For Level 5 the probability of availability could already be 0.99 and would remain there even if the loan period for this category was extended to ten years. For Level 4 the probability of availability might already be 0.8 with a loan period of four weeks and no further action us required. Availability for Level 3 items might be increased to 0.8 by reducing the length of the loan period from four weeks to three weeks. To reach 0.8 availability for Level 2, the length of the loan period may need to be reduced to two weeks. This leaves us with Level 1 items–the rather small number of highly popular items in the library. To ensure a probability of availability of 0.8 one might need, say, five copies of each and a loan period of one week.

Buckland (1975) has published data that show how popularity (level of demand for an item), length of loan period and number of copies affect the probability of availability of books. With a long loan period of ten weeks, the chance that one of the most popular books (class A) will be on the shelf, assuming a single copy, is only .37. This probability can be increased to .66 with two copies and .86 with three. On the other hand, reducing the length of the loan period, without buying further copies, also has a profound effect on the probability of availability. With a one-week loan period, even the most popular items in this hypothetical library have a high probability (.91) of being on the shelf when sought by a user. As Buckland's data show clearly, reducing the loan period or buying further copies are strategies that have most profound effects on the items in greatest demand. The actual probabilities of availability within this model would be determined by the different values accorded to the levels of popularity.

Buckland (1975) has reported that a type of "homeostatic" effect may govern book availability. That is, if satisfaction level is pushed up from, say 0.5 to 0.8, use the library may increase substantially because of improved expectations of success among the community. This greatly increased demand, however, increases competition for the library's resources and forces satisfaction level down–perhaps back to 0.5. Automated circulation systems allow one to conceive of a self–regulating library with no fixed loan period. An algorithm incorporated within the system would tell the user how long a particular book could be borrowed at the time of checkout. The calculation would be made on the basis of the circulation history of the book and the number of copies held, the loan period being calculated to ensure that the desired satisfaction level (say 0.8) will be maintained. The system would probably work with a large but finite number of loan periods–in the range of, say, five to ten. Of course, such a policy might not be popular with users, especially those who find that the several books they borrow on a particular day all have different return dates, but it would definitely make the library more efficient in terms of the probability of materials sought.

A somewhat different approach to the monitoring of collection development practices involves the comparison of a subject profile of what is being acquired with a subject profile of community interests or probable demands. This is most appropriate to the academic world, where it is possible to express the probable interests of a department in terms of the content of its curriculum, which may be converted into class numbers from the bibliographic scheme in use and the probable demand in terms of the size of the department (number of faculty, number of students, number of instructional units).

The profile of interest for the various departments can be matched against holdings, current acquisitions, or current circulation. Example of use of such techniques can be found in the work of McGrath, Golden and Jenks. McGrath (1968) showed, for each academic department, the number of circulated books relevant to the departmental profile, the percentage of the total circulation/enrollment ratio. Golden (1974) related the class numbers associated with a course to the number of books owned in these classes and to enrollment figures for the course in an attempt to identify strengths and weaknesses in the collection. Jenks (1976) compared circulation figures with the number of students in each department and with the number of books matching the profile of each department. He also ranked departments according to the use each made of that part of the collection matching its interest profile. Power and Bell (1978) propose a more elaborate formula that takes into account, for each academic department, the number of faculty members, the number of students at various levels, the holdings matching the departmental profile and circulation.

McGrath (1972) has shown that books matching the profile of institutional interests are much more likely to be borrowed than books not matching the profile, while McGrath et al. (1979) have used a subject classification approach to determine to what extent graduate and undergraduate students borrow books outside their own disciplines. Evans and Beilby (1983) describe collection evaluation through a sophisticated management information system employed within the libraries of the State University of New York. In one database were stored student enrollment figures classified by subject field according to the Higher Education General Information Survey (HEGIS) codes.

By using OCLC tapes, together with a conversion tape showing equivalencies between the HEGIS codes and Library of Congress class numbers, it was possible to relate the acquisitions data of a library to the enrollment. Thus, for each HEGIS code (e.g., 1103, German language), the system would generate a printout showing the number of titles acquired by the library, the percentage of the total acquisitions that this represents, the number of student credit hours and the percentage of the total credit hours that this represents.

Subject areas in which strong (or weak) relationships exist between student credit hours and acquisitions patterns can thus be identified and any necessary corrections made.

Kountz (1991) has performed similar analyses. Since student credit hours or credit units in various disciplines are reported to the U.S. Department of Education in the form of HEGIS or, now, IPEDS (Integrated Postsecondary Education Data System) codes and these codes can be converted into Library of Congress or Dewey Decimal class numbers, a profile of "constituency interests" can be matched against collection, acquisition or circulation data. Kountz uses titles per unit of student credit in the various subjects as a measure of the degree to which the collection matches interests. Similar analyses may also be possible in the special library environment. For example, Spaulding and Stanton (1976) and Kennedy (1983) describe the use of the Dewey classification as an aid to book selection in an industrial library network.

A selection profile for each member library is constructed, using DDC numbers plus verbal descriptions. Circulation data were used in the building of the profiles. Computer–generated reports allow a manager to determine to what extent materials purchased in a particular time period match a library's profile. While such analyses are not completely dependent on automated systems, it is obvious that they become more practical when the figures needed can be extracted from databases representing holdings, circulation or current acquisitions.

A significant collection management problem in the academic world is that associated with the equitable distribution of the materials budget over the interest of the various departments: how much should be spent on the acquisition of chemistry materials, how much on history, how much on education and so on?

The types of analyses discussed in the previous section can be useful in suggesting criteria for such allocation–

e.g., dollars allocated in proportion to student credit units. An allocation formula may be more easily justified if it takes into account a number of different criteria. Again, the development of allocation formulae is not dependent on automation. Nevertheless, many of the figures needed to develop a formula may be available from various databases and it is much easier to develop a multi–component formula when the component data can be manipulated by computer. While some justification can be made for any and all of these components, a formula that takes into account so many components may be too complex to apply in practice. The major problem involved is that of getting agreement on how much weight each .components should receive in the calculation of the allocation.

In general, it is based more on inputs to a department than on outputs. While instructional output can be considered to be reflected in number of students graduating, research output (e.g., in publications produced) are not considered at all. Brownson (1991) discusses the limitations of allocation formulae of the type that have been used in the past. He proposes a somewhat different approach based primarily on (1) the collection strength desired in a particular subject, (2) an estimate of the present strength in that subject, (3) the number if items owned in that class, (4) the circulation in that class and (5) extent of faculty research in the subject as reflected in number of research projects.

Ottensmann and Gleeson (1993) and Gleeson and Ottensmann (1993) have described an approach to the development of a budget allocation formula for a public library, based on data derived from a computerized circulation system. The objective is to allocate the budget in such a way as to optimize circulation "within the constraints of other objective established by librarians."

Various investigators have attempted to apply expert system techniques to the selection of materials for library collections. Rade et al. (1987) have described an expert system approach to the selection of journals. While their objectives were somewhat different the decision on whether or not a journal should be included in the MEDLARS database–the criteria built into their system (type of publisher, language, type of article, type of author, publication standards) would be among those relevant to a knowledge base designed to aid a librarian in journal selection decisions. Meador and Cline (1992) describe a workstation designed to make readily accessible all of the information that a librarian might need in selection decisions–collection development guidelines, holdings and circulation data, financial data and so on.

While not an expert system per se, this approach can be considered as a first step toward the development of such a system. Sowell (1989) describes a rudimentary expert system to aid in monograph selection, but he deals only in a very narrow subject area and the prototype developed was tested with very few cases.

4

Systems Study

With the advent of automation of library services and functions though smoothness and ease is felt but it has increased many complexities also. As such many new problems come up which a modern library and librarian have to face. A systems study is indispensable when a library faces these problems and admits that it is no longer serving its community effectively.

It is pertinent to note that "Systems study" is equated to the phrase "let's get organized." It is prerequisite to a well-designed and successful automated system but the results of such a study need not be an automated system.

Study methods and techniques can and should be used in analyzing, evaluating and designing all levels of data processing. The librarian familiar with the concepts and techniques of systems study should be able to increase the efficiency and productivity of the library even if the only available mechanical equipment is the computer.

What is Systems Study?

The systems study is defined as the logical analysis of the present systems; the evaluation of the efficiency, economy, accuracy, productivity, and timeliness of existing methods and procedures measured against the established goals of the library; and the design of new methods and procedures or modification of existing methods and procedures to improve the flow of information through the systems.

The main distinction between the analysis and design phases is that analysis is a rigorously controlled inquiry into existing conditions, while design is the resulting, synthesizing process in which new ideas are generated and refined. Design is the final phase of a systems study involving creative thinking, coordination of the conclusions reached in the analysis and deductive reasoning directed toward realization of the stated objectives and goals of management.

The concept of systems study consists of three interdependent phases:

1. *Analysis,* which is the accurate delineation of the requirements placed on a system; the current procedures by which the requirements are met; the outputs of the system in satisfaction of the system's requirements; and the inputs used to generate the outputs. The four items under analysis represent concurrent identification of the areas of inquiry, coupled with the charting of all operations, functions, decisions and actions, the gathering of data produced and forms used, the listing and evaluation of available personnel and equipment, all synthesized into a report of existing conditions.
2. *Evaluation,* which is the detailed examination of current procedures with respect to their adequacy to implement the mission of the system.
3. *Design,* which is the action taken by validation of the existing systems, by modification of it, or by

substitution of a newly designed system to satisfy the demands being placed on the system.

The use or terms in subsequent detailing of phases of a systems study can be a source of confusion. It is our intention here to avoid technical language as much as possible in order to serve better the understanding of the non-specialist. The simple terms chosen are applicable to processing by any means, manual or machine and can be expanded or modified where appropriate.

Goals: The objectives of the total system that establish demands placed against each system and its subsystems.

Demands: The established requirements of a system and its subsystems.

Requirements: The supply of data, information, action taken resulting from a demand.

Input: The printed form, written record, oral information, instructions needed to satisfy a requirement.

Output: The answer to the requirement of a system in the form necessary to convey or transmit information.

Subsystem: A major part, component, or activity of a system.

Operations: The major, specific units of work.

Procedures: Used synonomously with operations.

Jobs: Used synonomously with operations and procedures.

Elements of operations: The functions, decisions, actions comprising operations.

Functions: The processing steps in operations.

Decisions: The determination of the steps to be taken to complete a function.

Action: The course taken as a result of the decision.

It is suggested that the following terms are commonly in use and therefore can be helpful in effective interchange of ideas with management specialists. Further, the reader will note that the arrangement of the terms attempts to indicate their logical and hierarchial interrelationships.

Librarians and the Systems Study

It is remarkable that Intelligent staff participation and interest are essential to the success of any study to effect operating improvements in a system. In order to consolidate the gains that can come from a systems study the personnel must be capable of maintaining surveillance of the recommended operational structure and procedures. A systems study is the beginning for a different administrative and organizational work pattern that must be monitored in order to maintain and improve the library's ability to achieve the goals set for it. Regular analysis and evaluation of current methods and procedures should ensure that the demands for information and action being placed on the systems are being met. If they are not, the design and modification of methods and procedures become necessary because of the changing requirements of the system. Thus the need for the "new breed in librarianship," as Paul Wasserman puts it in his monograph "The Librarian and the Machine."

This "new breed" is the library systems analyst and the programming librarian. The presence of such personnel trained in the required managerial skills should release other professional librarians from processing functions to the areas of professional services to library users and to research in user requirements and improved methods of service. Basic education in librarianship coupled with specialization in data processing, or computer programming, or both, is suggested, if not essential for the professionally oriented library systems analyst and programming librarian.

As held by both Wasserman and Minder the problems to be solved are not simply tied to managerial technology also involve understanding of the professional objectives to be served. Librarians must be able to analyze, evaluate and design their own systems in terms of the requirements of librarianship. Otherwise the management and computer technologist, unaware or uncertain of the goals of librarianship, may adversely influence the organizational structure required for the attainment of the purposes of library service.

Again, as Wasserman writes in discussing the use of technological expertise by libraries, "The responsibility of the data processing person must be subordinate to a management which is broader and more comprehensive in its approach to the programme of the library. Even when those who are trained or experienced in data processing begin to assume general and broader library management responsibility, it must be for the ability which those so chosen manifest in these broader problems of organization than simply those tied to its technology."

Thus it seems advisable to look toward the library profession itself in the development of these new administrative positions in order to maintain balance in the composition of library administrative leadership. It would appear composition of library to have on its administrative staff at least one full-time officer whose responsibility is that of improving the library's systems and procedures and constantly modifying processes and procedures as demands or requirements placed on the organization change.

The size of a library is not a factor in the need for systems study. In the case of the "one-men" library it would be left for the librarian himself to acquire the requisite managerial skills. On the other hand the medium-to large–sized library organizations might well think in terms of full-time staff specialists.

Since the systems analyst or manager of systems and procedures is a staff officer, established and accepted as an agent of the library's director, his point of view and interest must be coterminous with those of the director.

The responsibilities of this position, in cooperation with library department heads, include the following functions:

1. Assisting management in the review and evaluation of operations and services to meet the established goals of the library.
2. Designing and implementing in cooperation with supervisory staff new or improved operating systems for increasing effectiveness, strengthening operating or management controls and expediting perfor-mance of routine work.
3. Developing operating manuals and reviewing, improving and planning statistical and accounting reports for managerial control at all levels.
4. Evaluating existing forms and as necessary designing new or improved forms.
5. Conducting training programmes for staff management in the regular application of systems study techniques to daily operating problems and in the capabilities and use of the computer in operations and library services.
6. Directing the design and programming of computer–based systems and representing the library's interests in shared computer facilities.
7. Keeping abreast of new developments in data processing, together with associated equipment and their application in library operations.

Library systems analysis, evaluation and design will be ineffectual unless done by persons who are trained or formally educated in librarianship. Although without experience, the library school graduate is prepared to learn the nuances of library service that can only be gained through experience. At least his schooling has made him aware of this contingency and he is prepared to develop professional attitudes.

This cannot be safely said of the one trained solely in managerial techniques. Library schools in the main are beginning to recognize the need for an introduction to systems study and data processing. A recent sampling of some half dozen schools revealed thinking in this direction. This is corroborated by Hayes' table of university programmes. There is, however, a tendency to feel that the student librarian without sufficient prior knowledge of the components of a total library system would not properly profit from instruction in these phases of managerial science.

Cannot this be said, too, of the student in such a course as "Library Administration" or "Library Organization," where the application of principles can only be inferred and likely misinterpreted in the case of the many students who have not even elementary exposure to the operation of a library? Paul Wasserman suggests that the library school should offer programmes in data processing to the practicing librarian at an intermediate level, "not necessarily tied to any formal degree level resulting in some type of certificate midway between the master's and doctorate.

Conversely it is suggested that programmes in the specific functions of the control systems of a library be offered to management degree holders. This can be done and is being done by some libraries through in-service study programmes. In institutions where both a library degree and a management degree are offered, an interdisciplinary programme could be profitable in making available to libraries management personal knowledgeable in library operations. Modern library management, aware of the need for system study, has no recourse but to learn the techniques and tools of systems study and the skills to apply them—the basis of good management.

If a library is to examine itself with the techniques of management science, the responsible personnel should be trained to do so. Because the systems study represents a demanding total library effort that may result in major operating changes, the entire library staff, under the strong leadership of the administration of the library, should be fully involved in planning and conducting the study.

Here the guidance, direction and personal participation of the director of the library are critical. He is responsible for the proper execution of the study.

Having received governing administrative authori-zation to proceed, the first responsibility of the director of the library is to select and appoint the staff to make the study. There are two principles to be kept in mind here: (*a*) a good systems study cannot be done on a part–time basis; and(*b*) the person selected to direct the study preferably should possess a combination of education in librarianship and training in the methods of systems analysis as taught in modern management courses. Since satisfaction of the latter prerequisite probably is not possible in most instances, one of two courses is open: either to release a library staff member from other duties to prepare himself for the conduct of a study, or, to bring in a skilled systems analyst unfamiliar with library organization.

Notably, the outside analyst skilled in modern management techniques should become fully familiar with the library's problems and responsibilities and develop a rapport and identification particularly with the supervisory staff. It is probable that the analyst from outside the library organization will require at least six months of intensive study and orientation to become sufficiently familiar with the library's problems and responsibilities and to develop rapport with the staff.

He should not approach the study with preconceived notions of the local problems to be solved, possibly arising from his work with another library or with what he feels is an analogous organization. Although the conditions he sees in a cursory inspection may appear to be the same as he has encountered before, the causes of the conditions to be studied frequently are completely different.

The analyst's responsibility is to determine *what* problems exist, *how* and *where* they originated and *how* the conditions at hand can be corrected.

The composition of the study staff should be as follows:

1. A library officer possessing responsibility and authority within the library's organization, to take supervision of the study.
2. At least one member of the study staff fully trained and experienced in the application of management-analysis techniques, preferably a librarian.
3. At least one member of the staff skilled in electronic data processing (EDP) methods, particularly if an automated system is contemplated; and again this member preferably should be a librarian.

4. Clerical assistance sufficient to support the work of the study staff.

It is conceivable that the requirements in Items 1-3 could be met by one person. However, it is more likely that two persons will be needed to meet the indicated requirements in the case of the medium– or large-sized libraries. A major factor here, of course, is that the library must continue to operate during the study and the dual responsibility could impede the progress of the study if only one person undertakes the role.

Identifying the Study Problems

The study staff is to develop with the library's management a detailed procedural plan and time schedule for the study, the first step of which is the general definition of the problems to be studied and the identification and description of the specific problems involved. It is the responsibility of the library's management to supply a clear and concise statement of these problems in the form of a *written report* such as would have been prepared for gaining governing administrative support and financing for the systems study originally. Problem definition must be in sufficient detail to serve as a guide to the study staff members and to inform the other members of the library's organization who are concerned with the activities named as areas to be covered by the study.

Long-Term Goals

The next step, critical in planning and conducting the study, is the definition of the library's overall goals, of which the systems study staff must be fully aware in relation to the problems to be studied. Goals are those factors that the management of the library determine to be important for accomplishment by the library. The statement of goals determines the major requirements resulting from demands that should be satisfied by the library through its data processing and informational systems.

Goals are basic in evaluating the current system and in designing a new system. If the goals are not precisely and correctly defined and understood in detail, the results can only be an inaccurate evaluation of current operations and the design of a faulty system. Therefore the study staff should verify the validity of the stated goals through discussion with library users, department heads in the library, department heads of the parent organization of the library and with the key administrative officers of the library's governing organization. Long-term planning is implicit in defining the library's goals. Because most libraries are in a period of dynamic and persistent growth, systems to satisfy long-term goals should be designed with the capability of handing increased demands.

Thus computer-based systems are suggested. Such systems have the capability of less costly and more efficient growth as demands on the library grow. Today's commonly applied manual systems often become more costly and less efficient under increasing demand and do not possess the "stand-by" qualities of the computer system in adjusting to growing requirements.

The following are some of the major goals of many libraries today:

(a) to improve service to users;

(b) to provide more prompt access and greater use of the library's resources; and

(c) to participate in library network programmes of

bibliographic data distribution and information transfer.

After the goals have been defined, the scope of the study must be established. Here the particular data processing systems within the library that are to be studied are identified as well as the organizational units in which the operations are performed and the activities involved in order to prevent wandering into other systems with which management is not concerned at this juncture; and within the system priorities are established for the components thought to need early attention by the library's administration. It is important in specifying scope and priorities that the systems study staff not be too rigidly restricted but rather allowed a degree of flexibility permitting recognition of other areas that might be affected by the particular system directly assigned for study.

Within the scope management also should define any limits or restrictions to be placed on the development of a system. It is important, obviously, for the study staff to know these parameters before the systems design phase. Illustrative of limits and restrictions are: (*a*) the type of system wanted: computer based or not computer based; (*b*) number and proportional distribution of personnel to be in the system; and (*c*) tolerable unit or total costs of operations of the system.

In further preparation the study staff members should decide on the methods and techniques to be used in the study for obtaining and recording the necessary information. These should be determined in order to assure a logical, systematic study and to permit comparison of findings within the systems. For example, if statistical work sampling is to be used, the confidence level to be accepted must be agreed on in advance with applicable sampling techniques being uniformly employed; survey forms must be designed for each of the surveys to be conducted; type and format of reports to be presented must be determined—that is, graphic reports such as organization charts, procedure flow charts, graphs, tables, and so forth; and written reports or other narrative materials must be agreed on.

Involved also in the methods used are designation of the persons to be interviewed, the records to be obtained and analyzed, the equipment available and its use and a detailed outline of the specific types of information to be sought. Adoption of uniform methods and procedures assures that the results reported by each study staff member are consistent in content and format and allow uniform comparison and evaluation by the staff in consultation.

As terminal planning steps the organization of the work of the study staff should be set down and a time schedule prepared for completion of its assignment measured by man-days or man-months; the types of skills needed for each assignment have to be determined—that is, managerial analysis, clerical, programming and so forth; the responsibilities of each person in prosecuting and completing his study assignment should be explicitly defined based on a list of specific identifiable study stages, each with a target date for completion; target dates for interim reporting to the library's management and to the study group as a whole should be set as well as the target date for submission of the final study report.

The time schedule is not only important to the orderly and expedi-tious prosecution of the study but also to administrative knowledge and acceptance of howlong current library operations will be slowed or otherwise adversely affected by the study's demands on the operating time.

Announcement of Study Plan

As the plan for the systems study is being formulated the director of the library should have introduced the idea to the library staff, indicating the reasons for the study and its objectives. Such announcement would include: (*a*) an indication of the reasons for the study; (*b*) a description of the principal goals of the study; (*c*) a description of the benefits expected; and (*d*) solicitation of the full cooperation of the members of the library staff, assuring them of their major roles and engendering their full support and interest in order that the study be successful. When the planning is completed, the director should review the finished plan with the study staff and with other members of the library's administration.

When he has approved the plan, the director of the library should make a formal announcement of the undertaking of the systems study to the community served by the library, indicating the reasons for the study and its objectives and anticipated benefits as well as explaining what problems the user of the library may temporarily encounter during the period of the study. The library staff should be reassured at this time of the administration's awareness and sympathetic under-standing of the disruption of each staff member's assigned duties and, further, be assured of the administration's firm support of the study.

It should be demonstrated to the staff that without the cooperation and participation of each member the study cannot lead to results beneficial to the staff and to the library.

Staff Training Programme

Following the announcement of the starting date of the study, it would be well to conduct a short staff training programme detailing the techniques used in a systems study. Discussion of these techniques should bring a better understanding of the study, generate the very necessary staff interest in it and furnish knowledge of what information the analyst will be seeking in his contacts with individual library staff members. The training programme also might well include description of the potential use and contribution of computers in library data processing operations and library services. At the same time the library staff should be provided with selected references to the current literature on library automation.

It cannot be overstressed that staff understanding, perceptiveness and support are prerequisite to a systems study resulting in practicable systems design. Support in this phase of organizational improvement efforts will be carried over into the successful implementation of the study's recommendations. As in any activity staff cooperation, willingness, interest, desire and pride in work generally assures attainment of operating objectives.

5

What is Systems Design?

> "One can no more develop capacity by resting on his job than he can learn to spell by sitting on a dictionary."
>
> —***Arthur Dean***

Having an understanding of some aspects of library systems, now we turn to principles of systems design.

Basically, in designing a new system the same data used in preparing the report of evaluation of the existing system are used in the design phase that culminates the systems study. The evaluation report obviously serves as the starting point or basis for the design of a new system, containing as it does suggestions for substantive changes by the analyst who at this point in the study should be conversant with the strengths, weaknesses, and unsolved problems in the present system and should be fairly well convinced about the corrective actions to be taken.

It is to be kept in mind that the goals and objectives of the library's management should be reviewed in relation to the requirements currently being placed on the library as well as in relation to the library's long-range plans of development and those of its governing administration. These goals, after being reaffirmed, amended, or changed, can be accepted as definite and the requirements of the existing system may be re-evaluated against them.

Are extant requirements still pertinent? Can specific requirements be changed if this is needed? Answers to such questions cannot be arrived at arbitrarily but should be developed in the light of pro and con views of the responsible staff members who are to make the new system operable.

Any desired changes in requirements controlled by outside sources would be subject to consultation with such sources.

After having a through review of goals next step in a systems design is assessment of its economic feasibility.

Economic Feasibility

Besides confirmation of the goals of the library the analyst should secure affirmation of the economic parameters that must be taken into account in designing the new system. If in his preliminary decisions about what corrective measures should be taken the analyst sees the feasibility of computer applications, will the library and its governing administration approve the additional cost of electronic data processing including the cost of peripheral equipment needed for library computer-based operations?

If additional personnel is suggested for increased productivity and elimination of chronic backlogs of work, is the administration prepared to meet the increased operating costs? These and similar factors of increased costs should be delineated before attempting the design of the system if it is to result in one fitted to stated cost limitations rather than one providing an apparently ideal solution. In evaluating a proposed new system management's decision to accept it is strongly influenced by cost of installation and operation; that is, staffing, equipment, space, new forms, and other expense items.

Consequently the proposal to management must include a comparison of the total and, more important, the unit operating costs of the current system with the projected costs of the proposed new system; it must also include the conversion expense and any capital expenses entailed in remodelling and expanding working space. The cost of changing over from a current system to a new or modified one are always significant and often are not sufficiently analysed and evaluated for valid managerial decision. Estimated time (costs) and the cost of units of new equipment to be blended with existing equipment required for conversion are necessary in any case but entirely imperative in the case of converting to computer-based operations.

Underestimation of the time needed for records' conversion and the auxiliary equipment and staff required may lead to considerable embarrassment and even to failure in implementing the proposed system. As an illustration of the seriousness and impact of the time-cost factor, let us assume that the analyst recommends and management concurs in the adoption of a computer-based cataloging system for the library.

Such a decision can be ill founded unless supported by an estimate of the comparative cost of continuing the cataloging by traditional methods and the cataloging by computer-assisted methods; and it should be further supported not only be an estimate of the cost of converting the present catalogue records for a beginning base book catalogue but also by a projected estimate of the annual costs to be incurred in keeping the machine readable record up to date and the book catalogs in print and cumulated. In recommending any computer-based system it should be realized that the conversion of man-readable records to machine-readable records may be the most expensive aspect of the programme.

The next most expensive factor generally is the printing and publishing of the machine output. It is, incidentally, these two factors that call for application of the principle that machine records should contain only data clearly essential to meeting the library system's require-ments. To continue with the illustration the analyst can readily make a close estimate of the annual cost of personnel, supplies, and other expense items incurred in the existing cataloging operations. The proposed computer-based system contains the same cost elements but with the addition of programming; personnel, who may be staff members available because of discontinued manual functions, for preparing the computer input; purchase or rental of in-house input machinery; subscription to the Library of Congress MARC magnetic tapes; computer processing time; and the printing and binding of the cumulating catalogue records during the year.

Programming costs are usually very difficult to estimate, mainly due to two factors: (i) the individual programmer's ability and knowledge of library requirements; and (ii) the complexity of catalogue filing and catalogue data. Computer processing costs will very with the programmes execution time in producing a required listing.

To a considerable degree the computer time costs will be affected by the preciseness of the programmes logic and the size of the data base. In estimating the printing and binding costs dependence may be placed on a printing house representa-tive. It can be anticipated that annual cataloging personnel charges will remain approximately the same. Supplies and expense items including new equipment rental or amortiza-tion, except for on-line input devices, will tend to be less than in a manual system.

The estimated additional annual operating costs are offset by savings such as lesser cataloging costs up to the computer-connected operations; elimination of the need to purchase additional catalogue cases as the collection grows; the freeing of centrally valuable floor space taken up by the catalogue cases; elimination of the prepara-tion of duplicate sets of catalogue cards for departmental and subject-area catalogs; the possible sale of printouts from the MARC tapes to regional institutions as aids in cataloging, current book selection, and collection evaluation; the processing of books more speedily to the shelves; the saving of the time of library users and the staff with the printed book catalogs being available at various points within and outside the library; and the possible sale of the printed book catalogs to other libraries. Referring again to estimation of the extraordinary annual expense of computer processing and press printing of book catalogs during the year, the yearly pattern of printout and publication consistent with adequate service to readers must be determined—monthly, quarterly, four-month, or semiannual cumulations.

The monthly cumulation pattern obviously is the most costly although it does provide near-maximum user utility outside of on-line accessibility to the catalogue data in the computer data base. The cost of the monthly pattern will be found to be in the order of twice as great as that for any other of the alternates. It further will be found that the variation in cost among the quarterly, four-month, and semiannual cumulations is not significant.

Although less convenient to the user than the monthly cumulation, the quarterly pattern including two noncumulated monthly catalogs in each quarter results in the reader having to consult from two to a maximum, of five printed catalogue listings until the annual cumulation is supplied. The costs of converting and printing the existing catalogue records as the basic book catalogue in the "start-up" of the computer-based system represent an extraordinary one-time expense with no offset savings over manual cataloging methods because the card catalogue must be maintained until the base catalogue is printed and published.

The costs to be estimated here include the cost of preparing and "loading" the catalogue data into the computer, the cost of computer processing, and the cost of press printing the base catalogue in the edition size found to give the most effective service to users. Preparation costs of catalogue records for the computer include estimation of the hourly rates of there cords' input keying operation, proofreading, and correcting, as well as an estimate of the time required for inputting the records into the computer. To complete the analysis of the cost involved in his recommendation to install the computer-based cataloging system, the analyst using the cost data gathered to this point should prepare a five or six-year calendar of computer and publishing costs including the one-time base catalogue cost in the first year of the operation of the computer-based system.

A pattern of catalogue cumulation must be proposed: single-year cumulations to the fifth year when a five-year cumulation would be produced; annual cumulations on a year-to-year basis; or other patterns judged appropriate to the economic capabilities of the library and that will give adequate service to users. Given an anticipated annual average acquisitions rate and using currently prevailing personnel and machine costs, the analyst can extend this analyst over a period of years showing that the annual costs of records' conversion, computer processing, and press print will remain more or less constant.

It, however, can be anticipated in a computer-based cataloging system, that net annual costs will be greater by approximately 25 per cent than those incurred in following conventional manual procedures, excluding any of the possible offsets mentioned earlier.

Obviously, an analysis such as that described above should be undertaken for all proposed computer-based systems if the governing administration is to reach a valid decision on whether or not to adopt computer-based methods for the library. Computer-based or noncomputer-based systems design should be validated by analysis of the time-cost factors involved. A major factor in management's decision to accept a newly designed system will be the improved ability to satisfy the system's requirements. This improvement may be beneficial to a related system within the library, to a coordination of systems, to library users, and to manage-ment decision making.

Although these benefits are usually too intangible to be measured in dollars and cents, they should be submitted in justification of costs. For example, improved service to library users, improved quality, timeliness and form of information and reports required for decision and action, and improved coordination of operations among systems may be cited to justify a computer-based circulation system.

Unit Costs

Basically, the cost of the processing of each unit of material in each system is necessary in a comparison of the total operating cost of the former systems with that of a newly designed one. Comparative total costs do not supply management with a basis for making a decision to accept the proposed system. Determination of the cost of processing one book order, of cataloging one title, of discharging one book, or of processing a similar work unit of a system, correlated with the standard processing a similar work unit of a system, correlated with the standard rate of processing each unit, should yield meaningful total costs' comparison in relation to the rated capacity of the old system and the required capacity of the new.

Therefore, management can decide to accept increased total operating costs, aware that a stated requirement for increased productivity legitimately causes the differential in operating costs. This discussion on unit cost of processing is confined to the major cost factor of directly chargeable personnel within a given system. While this, in general, is sufficient for establishing unit costs, it may be refined and in certain cases should be: for example, the shared use of workers between systems with each chargeable at a prorated cost and the shared use of equipment whose rental and operating costs also are proportionately chargeable.

Essentials of Design Phase

The design phase of the systems study includes nearly all the elements of the analysis phase, varying only in objective and approach. It will be recalled that in the analysis phase a beginning was made by determining the procedures and methods currently employed by the system, followed by analyses of the requirements, outputs, and inputs found in the system.

In the design phase the beginning process is validation or determination of the requirements to meet management's goals, validation or revision of the system's outputs, and validation or change of controllable inputs. Based on the results of these decisions new operating procedures are promulgated to fit the needs of the system in meeting its requirements.

Thus the order to approach in system design is verification of requirements and then specification of the system's inputs/outputs. Greenwood supplies a thorough outline of the analyst's tasks in designing systems. There is also a strong element of parallelism between the design and the evaluation phases. In evaluating current operating procedures and methods the analyst is observing and seeking evidence of the efficacy as well as the inadequacy of applied procedures and methods. In the process and as a logical by-product he is gradually formu-lating and substantiating his ideas for needed change, revision, or scrapping of specified procedures, anticipating the design of a new system. Directed to design a new system the analyst retraces his steps through the system in the evaluation phase. He checks his findings and prepares specific recommendations for recasting procedures for organisational structure and job descriptions, for redesigning forms and reports, and for improving working-space conditions.

Why New Design?

It is significant to note that among the several objectives in designing a system perhaps the major one is planning for all functions of a system to logically fall within the purview of the system. Other important objectives are that there be correlation and interdependence of all functions, subsystem to subsystem and worker to worker; that similar correlation exist in the preparation and maintenance of records and files and that necessary duplication of records and files be eliminated; and that the systems' activities be performed in a logically sequential mode, organised physically for the smooth flow of work through the system.

Another significant objective in systems design is definition of the authority needed by the head of the system as well as by the supervisors under him in order that all staff members may make the decisions and take the actions indigenous to the operating effectiveness of the system.

Corollary to this objectives the analyst should designate the one supervisor to whom certain workers in a system are to report. The establishment of this relationship is necessary to prevent worker disorientation and the consequent hampering of the orderly flow of work designed into the system. Having a knowledge of the primary requirements of the system the analyst-designer should specify what ancillary requirements, if any, are to be met and the outputs necessary to satisfy all the requirements placed on the system. For each new or modified requirement and output a new or corrected worksheet for each requirement and output should be filled out as fully as possible.

Although the some worksheet forms are used, the difference lies in the analyst's approach. Here he is specifying the requirements to be met and the outputs to be prepared in meeting those requirements instead of simply recording the status quo of requirements and outputs called for in the initial analysis of current methods and procedures. If the new design is restricted to available capabilities in the present staff, procedures should be designed to fit these capacities and levels of ability. It is particularly important that procedures be as routine as possible in order to limit the disruptive effect of any exceptions in the preparation of data and records standard to the system's operations.

The same is true if the new design is to make use only of available equipment. If restricted to the use of typewriters by budgetary exigencies, for example, there is no point in designing a system to exploit the characteristics of a paper-tape typewriter or key punch.

Manuals of Procedures and Operations

A cardinal principle in designing a system is that all procedures developed should be put in writing. As procedures for each operation are developed they should be described in sequential detail in writing, tested and supported by flow charts graphically illustrating the procedural steps, in each operation. These detailed descriptions of the procedural to be followed in the various operations are, of course, the basis of integrated manuals of procedure covering the system's major activities and fixing the logical flow of work through the system. It is constructed to reflect the administrative structure of the organization, the procedures within operations, and the forms used with a record retention policy statement for each form. The programme, policy, and procedure for processing the library's photocopying office charge accounts are outlined in detail.

The design of appropriate manual procedures is a principal prerequisite in the design of any type of system whether it involves electronic data processing or not. In any case and even in the most competent of computer-based systems there is substantial use of manual procedures in gathering information, in preparing this information as input to the computer system, and, as necessary, in processing the outputs to satisfy the requirements to be met by the system.

In designing the system, however, it is essential to know whether methods and procedures will be based on the use of common business machine aids or on the use of the computer and peripheral machine aids. The analyst should be thoroughly familiar with the various types of business machine that can be used in support of sound manual procedures in a system employing punched card, paper-tape, accounting, or copying equipment. At the same time he should be conversant with the techniques of computer-based systems as well as the supporting manual equipment compatible with computer input/output operations. Manual procedures systematically and logically developed for achieving maximum efficiency in an on computer-based system should supply satisfactory basis for building a computer-based system should this become feasible in the future.

At that time programmers will need to reana-lyze in minute detail procedures considered adaptable to computer manipulation for instructing the computer in the step-by-step accomplishment of tasks in substitution for manual processes.

Procedures Criteria

Good procedures possess certain characteristics that should be kept in mind in the course of designing a system. As the analyst develops procedures for implementing a system he should raise the following questions about each:

1. Does it furnish the outputs needed in satisfaction of stated requirements of the system?
2. Does each step in the procedure have a definite purpose in the generation of the output? Is it clearly necessary?
3. Does each function in the procedure move the item being processed one step nearer its completion as an output of the system?
4. Are operations staffed to achieve balance among procedural steps resulting in a smooth work flow and prevention of bottlenecks?

5. Are non-routine processing steps reduced to a minimum with a path minimizing disruption and delay provided for any exceptions?
6. Are available mechanical aids used to the extent possible in satisfying the objectives of the procedure?
7. Are the forms used in the procedure so designed as to supply data in a logical format common to related functions and systems, saving time of execution and obviating annotation in their flow through the system?

Satisfaction of the criteria implied in these questions is fundamental to the successful flow charting of the procedures.

The analyst in the course of the inputs/outputs survey has gathered samples of all the forms used and by the time he begins the design of the new system he will have decided on the forms or copies of forms to be eliminated, changed in format, and created. Because forms are the means of transmitting information and storing and avoiding repetitive transcription of information, the importance of the proper design in data processing is obvious. It is equally important that the form be designed for convenience and time saving in its preparation and use. The impact of the time lost in working with ill-designed forms is also obvious.

The design and redesign of forms is influenced and guided by several requirements and decisions.

1. Does the form provide for the recording of information in an itemized order consistent with the logical ordering of the elements of information recorded, permitting the most convenient preparation and use of the information at the least cost?

2. Does the form best serve the reciprocal and correlative characteristics of recorded data? In illustration of both Items 1 and 2 the book request form should be designed for recording bibliographic data during the preorder search in itemized progression standard to bibliographic entry; it should serve both for the purposes of ordering a book and for being a record for the originator of the request—thus indicating a two-part form.

The book ordering form should provide for itemized arrangement of data in the exact format of the book request and should be in multi parts to serve as an order slip, vendor's packing slip, in-process slip, request slip for Library of Congress cards, the on-order record in the public catalogue, and the notice slip to the originator of the request notifying him that the order has been received.

3. How will the form be prepared? If it is to be handwritten, item spacing must be sufficiently generous to avoid unintelligible abbreviations and crowding of characters. If it is to be machine prepared, machine spacing and consistency of item starting points permitting maximum use of the tabular setting should be designed into the form.

If both handwriting and machine preparation are involved, the form's design should be flexible enough for both methods. A principle here is the minimizing of handwritten data, confining it to the checking of boxes next to specified information printed on the form. The use of check boxes wherever possible not only speeds preparation and use of the form but may also improve the accuracy of the record due to the simplicity of checking a specific box.

4. Will the form be the basis for a temporary or permanent data file? Standardized size should be adopted

fitting the filing equipment usually available in a library. If a sheet form is required, it should be designed with adequate binding margins, punched if for ring binders, and specified in standard size for economy in printing and photocopying.

5. How many copies of the form are really needed to transmit information? For example, a requirement to be satisfied by the cataloging system is notifying the request or of a book that it has been received and is ready for his use. The copy of the book ordering form used for ordering Library of Congress cards is returned and is used to notify the request or reducing the multi part form by one.

6. Should commercially available stock forms be adopted? The adoption of such a form more frequently than not necessitates compromises when applying the from to local informational needs. Apparent savings in the purchase of stock forms can result in increased costs of processing.

Forms designed to meet the data needs for specific inputs/outputs of a given system are more economical, useful, and efficient than standardized forms designed for routine and purportedly common applications. Forms should not be regarded as inviolable but should be constantly re-evaluated with respect to their usefulness and ease of preparation. Whenever justified, they should be redesigned and replaced for more economical processing that will more than offset the cost of new ones and the discard of the inventory of the old.

7. What are the criteria in designing the multipart form? The first factors to be considered are the reciprocal and correlative characteristics of the data to be carried be

the form—that is, the number of copies to be transmitted to other points.

If such a multipart form is indicated, it should be printed in a continuous perforated strip for economy in processing achieved by elimination of repeated machine insertions and alignments. The advantages and disadvantages of carbon inserts and self-carbon papers should be studies, as well as the stubbing of the continuous form by adhesive, stapling, and other means for holding the alignment of copies. For example, in machine operations stapling can prove injurious to the equipment as well as cause misalignment of copies of the form. The arrangement of the multipart form should allow sequential extraction of copies in the order of the uses to be made of them. Further, the arrangement of copies should provide for the distribution of the original and the clearest carbon copies to the points where the data are used most. If instructions relating to certain parts of the form are needed, these spaces should be referenced to the instructions by number or other coding.

The use of different coloured copies of the multipart form should be investigated for identifying the origin of the form. If a copy of a form is to be mailed, it should be designed for insertion in a window envelope.

8. Is the form clearly understandable? The form in all its copies should be identified by headings clearly indicating the particular purpose and use of each copy. The exact data to be entered in the form should be self-explanatory. For purposes of routine distribution the various copies should be identified by numbers, bold-printed titles, or different colours of paper stock. As required the form should carry on its face or verso printed instructions for its preparation or use.

It can be surmised from the foregoing considerations and decisions in the design or redesign of forms, the following elements should be sought: clarity of layout requiring a minimum of printed instruction; handwriting held to a minimum with checking of printed captions maximized to reduce errors and save time in entering information; arrangement of items in a sequence parallel with the func-tions to be performed; appropriate spacing for convenient entry of the required informational; and a size for easy handling and for economy in printing, preparing, photocopying, filing, and mailing. The design or redesign of forms is an inescapable task in the design of a new system. The function of the analyst is to apply the principle that the same data or information should be recorded one time only and used by means of multiple parts at various points in the system.

Although the captioning of forms and the sequential arrangement of their itemization and arrangement of copies for distribution are functions of the analyst, he usually can depend on the sales representative of a reputable business forms and systems house to furnish a large measure of assistance.

The representing acts as a catalyst by again thinking through the purpose and arrangement of the form with the analyst, often suggesting improvements and refining phrases and captions. The representative also accepts responsibility for such mechanical features as the substance and quality of the paper stock in relation to whether the form will receive a large volume of use, be filed, or be discarded; the best copy duplicating method in relation to the machine used in executing the form; the use of single or continuous forms in relation to frequency and method of preparation; and most important the sales representative will see to the drafting of the form and its proper design for efficient preparation and use by the methods and machines employed by the library.

The principles of design discussed in this chapter apply in the design of a computer-based system, varying only in the precision, logic, clarity, standardization, and specificity of information to be acted on and the anticipated decisions to be implemented by the computer. The following outline indicated the areas with which the analyst should be concerned in designing a computer-based system.

1. *Characteristics of Available Computer System:* Most libraries cannot justify the cost of maintaining a computer system for their exclusive use. Therefore it can be anticipated that most libraries will be faced with designing their operating systems to fit the capabilities of available outside equipment. The characteristics and availability of such equipment should be know:
   (*a*) Means of input (punched cards, paper tape, telecommunication).
   (*b*) Means of storage (magnetic tape, disk, drum, core memory).
   (*c*) Storage capacity.
   (*d*) Means of output (printout, punched cards, magnetic tape, cathoderay tube).
   (*e*) Relative speed of machine components.
   (*f*) Computer time available for library operations.
   (*g*) Available "off-line" equipment (sorter, tabulator, interpreter).
2. *Generalized Systems Chart*: A diagram showing the following should be made:

(*a*) The primary input and output.

(*b*) The major activities of the system.

(*c*) The interdependence among the various systems.

3. *System Requirements Analysis:*

(*a*) Analyse requirements in terms of a computer-oriented system, keeping in mind that through programming the computer system can be assigned many of the routine decisions found at all levels of management.

(*b*) Analyze for all possible applications of the principle of management by exception, determining and designing reporting systems best serving management's needs.

4. *Inputs/ Outputs*

(*a*) Determine the input/output information required to satisfy the system, taking advantage of the speed of the computer.

(*b*) Evaluate inputs/outputs of the present system and determine what additional inputs/outputs are required and/or what inputs/outputs are not required; determine the minimum essential information.

5. *Decisions*

(*a*) Identify each decision required for successfully meeting the system's requirements.

(*b*) Identify those decisions that may be delegated to the computer mention, identify the responsible person.

(*c*) Identify the source records and reports from

which the information is obtained for making each decision.

6. *Input Media*

(*a*) Evaluate existing forms or design new ones as required to capture needed data.

(*b*) Determine within the characteristics of available computer equipment the machine-readable media best adapted to the system's requirements (punched cards, paper tape).

(*c*) Evaluate and select equipment to be used in the library to generate machine-readable input records (key punch, tape typewriter).

7. *Computer Storage and Output Media*

(*a*) Determine media best suited for computer reports—for example, punched card, magnetic tape, printout, microfilm, within the limitations of available equipment.

(*b*) Determine for each record the type of computer storage media required for efficient processing (sequential or random) within the capabilities of available equipment, such as magnetic tape, data cell, disk, or drum storage.

(*c*) Evaluate and select any equipment to be used in the library to store and process computer output to yield records and reports, such as an electronic accounting machine for punched cards.

8. *Functions*

(*a*) Identify each function required for successfully meeting the system's requirements.

(*b*) Determine those functions to be performed

under programmed control and those under manual control.

(*c*) Detail the procedures to be followed in the performance of each function.

9. *Resulting Actions*

(*a*) Identify the actions to be taken as the result of each decision.

(*b*) Identify the functions or further decisions resulting from each action.

The study staff should prepare the flow chart of the new system in sufficient detail: (i) to furnish guidance for the programming of the computer-based parts of the system, and (ii) to permit preparation of detailed instructions for the manual procedures of the system. The study staff should continually modify the computer-based system until the system's objectives are realized. An acquisitions system to illustrate major aspects of computer-based systems design principles.

> Final steps in the design of a computer-based or non-computer-based system are to:
>
> 1. Estimate the cost of installing the new system and its operating cost.
> 2. Compare the cost of the old system with that of the new.
> 3. Determine the staffing requirements of the new system.
> 4. Prepare a summary report for the library's management outlining the features of the new system in relation to the old.
> 5. Prepare a detailed procedural manual and time schedule for conversion to and installation of the new system.

The responsibility of the analyst should not end with the completion of the design phase of the systems study. The installation of the newly designed system should also be done by the systems analyst in cooperation with the line supervisor.

It is logical that the installation should be the responsibility of the analyst since he designed the system, is aware of the nuances of his design, and has a definite interest in seeing that the system starts up successfully. The analyst should coordinate and correlate the various factors entering into the implementing of new system—such as staff training, new forms, new equipment, and new facilities—so the installation can proceed according to a realistic time schedule.

For example, the installation of a computer-based circulation system could involve coordinating the preparation and procurement of machine-readable identification cards, punched cards for books, data collection devices, computer programmes, and new computer-produced forms such as overdue and recall notices. There are three possible ways in which a system may be installed: (i) all at once on a crash programme basis with title, if any, break in service during the transition; (ii) *simultaneously* as a parallel programme with both the old and the new system being concurrent for a predetermined time; and (iii) *step by step* on a piecemeal basis where portions of the new system are implemented within the old system. The size and nature of the new system will have considerable bearing on what installation approach the analyst may take.

For example, it may be possible to implement a punched-card circulation system step by step. The preparation and insertion of the punched cards in the books may be accomplished on a piecemeal basis: that is, as books circulate punched cards could be made up and then be inserted when the books are returned. When a sizable portion of the active collection has been covered, the switch over to the punched card system could then be made. The simultaneous type of installation, although expensive, may be feasible where assurance that a new system will perform as accurately as the old is desired. This would be particularly true in accounting operations where the new system's tallies should correspond with those produced under the old system.

The all-at-once approach may be used if a new operation is not considered complex, such as the use of photocopying machines to reproduce catalogue cards. The programme could be operational almost immediately after the card stock is available, the copier installed, and the staff trained.

After installing the system the analyst should plan to check back on its progress. This is essential if he is to obtain on-site feedback about the system so that he in cooperation with the line supervisor can make any necessary revisions and adjustments in operations, forms, and staffing. The analyst's follow-up report may also serve to justify and increase managements confidence in the new system.

The appropriate time to make the follow-up survey will vary with the situation. In any event it may be well to audit the system a month after it has been declared operational. After this initial observation, it also may be well to have a review of the system annually.

The follow-up report should not be done at a distance but by visiting the system and speaking with the staff and checking whatever controls may have been built into the system. For example, the statistics being kept in the new system may have been designed to reflect the effectiveness of the new system over the old. Reports on costs, unit production, and usefulness of equip-ment may be of value in the follow-up evaluation. Another method of testing quality control would be for the analyst to discreetly observe the progress of units through the system.

6

Automated Serials System

One california librarian firmly asserted that she is so utterly opposed to censorship that "when someone complains about a book in our library, I just put the book aside in a locked room, Right now we have two thousand books locked away like that."

Practically designing a computer-based serials system follows the prescribed pattern: the establishment of requirements, the provision of forms and the determination of the manual and machine procedures that will satisfy the requirements.

It is remarkable that primary requirement of the serials system is to provide users with an accurate and current file of the library's serials holdings including all the necessary bibliographic information. In the instance we shall discuss, the file will be a union catalogue containing the data required on all serials in both the general library and the branch libraries. The data in this file should be available not only in the general library but also in branches and to other possible users. Second, the system should be able to provide the means whereby the user as well as the library staff may request and receive within a reasonable time special catalogs or reports of the serials holdings by such categories as call number, language, and subject: and it should also provide special listings by publishers, vendors, types of serials, status (such as active, inactive), and by all condition of receipt (gift, purchase, or exchange).

Third, the system should be able to guarantee that all issues not received by the library will be claimed promptly and on a set schedule and also that the renewal of all serial subscriptions will be controlled by the system. Fourth, the system should be able to predict the time of receipt of a journal issue with accuracy thereby establishing a positive control over the timely receipt of all issues. Fifth, the system must be able to maintain and control all the accounting records necessary for its own internal use and be able to report to the comptroller the information required for payment of invoices. Sixth; the system should be able to provide the binding department with necessary information and records for those journals that are to be bound. It also should be able to provide such information and records on a scheduled basis in order to maintain an even workload for the binding staff.

Finally, the serials system should have the ability to handle the many changes that occur in the various serials titles.

With the establishment of the requirements of the system the next task is to determine what information is necessary as input to the computer system if it is to satisfy the requirements as outlined. It should be determined where this information can be obtained if existing records are inadequate and what format and under what restrictions the input of information should be placed. The input worksheet should be designed to obtain the maximum amount of information with the least cost. The form finally adopted should contain all the information necessary for the functioning of the system.

Procedure for Compiling

Remarkably, original step in compiling the serials record starts when the compiler removes from the existing central serials file the holdings record, or the current check-in record, or both. The holdings card indicates any title changes or title variations. If changes have occurred, the compiler removes from the central serials file those cross-referenced records pertaining to the title variations or changes in question; that is, all of the library's records covering the history of this particular title are removed.

Referring to the serials control record worksheet, the first box in the upper left-hand corner carries the Dewey call number obtained from the library's record. In the case of the call number, where there have been title changes or there are multiple subscriptions and the same call number has been used for each new change or subscription, it is necessary for the compiler to add to the call number a hyphen and an additional digit (–1, –2, –3, and so forth) to identify each title within the computer record. The next step in compilation is to verify the official title, if possible, in the *National Union Catalogue* (NUC).

If it is found there, it is used as the main entry for input to the computer. The LC call number, if found in NUC, is recorded in the upper right-hand corner of the form. The compiler also indicates under the word "verified" the volume and year of NUC in which the title was verified. If the publication is not found in NUC, the next step is to search in the *Union List of Serials.*

Here again, if the title is found, the entry is accepted as the main entry. If the entry is not found in the *Union List of Serials*, the search is continued in *New Serials Titles* and if necessary, in *Ulrich's International Periodicals Directory.* The next item on the form is the short title which cannot exceed forty characters in length. The short title should conform to the title as it appears on the cover of the serial itself as an aid to checking in the issue. The abbreviations for periodical literature provided by the United States of American Standards Institute are used in establishing the short title. Proceeding down the form the next blocks are Holdings- start and Holdings-end.

This information is obtained from the library's holdings record. The information for the Publication-start and Publicationend blocks is obtained from NUC or the *Union List of Serials* and if not located, it is taken from other bibliographic sources.

The items in the next two horizontal lines of data are coded. The following defines the data elements and supplies examples of some of the code structure.

Keyword	*Description of Data Element*
LIB (Library)	Refers to the particular library or collection that maintains the file of a journal (00 = general library, 41 = business and economics).
LOC (Location)	The location in the library. This is used primarily to indicate where the journal is to be shelved (2 = current display rack). It is also used to identify the location to which it is routed previous to shelving (A = table of contents photocopy service).
LANG (Language)	The language or languages in which the journal is published (01 = Chinese, 20 = multilingual with English).
TYPE	Refers to form of publication—that is, abstracts, periodicals, transactions (10 = index or abstract, 40 = proceedings).
STAT (Status)	Refers to variations such as active, ceased publication, discontinued subscription, title change (1 = ceased publication).
RET (Retention)	Refers to the period of time of retention

	and conditions under which a journal is kept, that is, one year and discard, two years in branch and forward to general library, and similar variations in handling (3 = discard after three years).
BIND (Bindery)	Refers to the commercial binder used.
COLOR (Colour)	The four-digit code for the color of binding cloth to be used.
ISSUE PHY VOL (Issues per physical volume)	Defines the number of issues that are bound in a physical volume.
INDEX	Refers to when and how the index is received and where it is found in the journal (0 = no index, 4 = separate, free on request).
INDEXED IN	Obtained from *Ulrich's International Periodicals Directory*. Here is indicated indexing services in which the journal is indexed or abstracted (175 = *Reader's Guide*, 095 = *Fuel Abstracts*).
FREQ (Frequency)	Defines the frequency of publication of each title- that is, monthly, weekly, quarterly, and so forth (01 = weekly, 16 = bimonthly).
NO. OF ISSUE VOL	The number of issues per bibliographic volume.
CC (Claim Control)	Indicates the waiting period at end of which an issue is claimed (21 = one month late).
JFMA.... (Jan, Feb, Mar, Apr)	Used for forecasting the time of receipt of issues so that the computer can produce the check-in punched card in advance of receipt.
REC (Receipt)	The condition of receipt— for example, gift, group purchase, membership, group purchase, exchange (4 = gift, 9 = group purchase.
GROUP NO.	If, for example, a journal is received as part of the package plan with the American Chemical Society, a unique two-digit number

	is assigned to American Chemical Society and each title received in the package plan is assigned that number so that all journals received under the plan can be identified as a group for accounting purposes.
DATE START	Refers to the date that the last subscription started and controls the renewal of the subscription.
LAST PAYMENT	Used to verify that a title was renewed previously and when.
SUB LGT (Subscription length)	Used in conjunction with DATE START to determine next renewal date of a title.
REQ DEPT (Requesting department)	Used in connection with the FUND NO for accounting and statistical purposes. The LIB codes are used in identifying departments that have requested subscriptions either for housing in the departments or in the general library.
FUND NO. (Fund number)	Refers to the account against which the subscription is charged.
SUBS PRICE (Subscription price)	Refers to the cost of a subscription or last renewal.
ISSUING AGENCY	Full name and address of the issuing agency (publisher).
SUPPLIER	The name and address of the supplier or vendor when different from the issuing agency.

The balance of the serials control record worksheet is used for the additional bibliographic control data desired in this system. Entered in the last part of the form are the S-SUBJECT entries as found in NUC for each title. If the title is not found in NUC, the librarians revising the records must assign at least one compatible subject to each title.

The A-ADDED entries used are those given in NUC excluding the added entry for editor.

Indication of title changes follow the subject and added entries. If there is a title change with the new title continuing old volume numbering, such title change is designated F-FORMERLY ISSUED AS, or C-CONTINUED AS. On the other hand a title change with its own and new volume numbering is designated Z-SUPERSEDES or X-SUPERSEDED BY. If two titles are merged to form a new title, both titles would be entered under the code M-MERGED.

Remarkably, any necessary notes that will facilitate the user's approach to a serial title are entered under the code N-NOTES. After the information has been compiled on the serials control record worksheets, it must be verified and, if necessary, revised. No information is sent to the data processing operator until it has been (necessarily reviewed and revised.

Procedures and Equipment in Generating Computer Input Record

After the data on the worksheet have been revised and all corrections made, it is forwarded to the data processing operator who prepares the input tape using the paper-tape typewriter. Reading from the serials control record worksheet the data processing operator types this information on a serials control record form simultaneously producing paper tape containing all of the compiled information.

It is significant to note that there are three ways of correcting information entered into the paper tape:

(i) If a character is incorrectly typed, the operator immediately may insert a delete character to erase the error and continue with the typing.

(ii) The operator at any time during the typing of a record may insert a special code which will indicate to the computer that this record is to be disregarded and that a substitute record will be entered.

(iii) At the end of the record the operator has the opportunity to correct any field that may have been typed in error by inserting the field control number followed by the correct information; a computer programme will then insert the corrected information furnished by the operator, in the field indicated.

Each serials control record form produced concurrently with the paper tape is proofread for typographical errors at the end of the day's production. Any errors that are found during proofreading may be corrected by the operator at any time. The correction procedure is to punch five items into the paper tape; first, the code indicating to the program that this is a correction record; second, a code indicating the type of correction (A for an addition to a record, C for a correction to some field within the record, or D to delete some item of information from the record); third, the Dewey call number of the title to be corrected; fourth, the field control number of the field in error; and fifth, the corrected information. The correction record on paper tape will be used to make the necessary corrections, additions, or deletions to the machine- readable record identified by the Dewey call number.

Design of Computer—Serial Record Load System

Requirements of the system are: (i) to produce a report for verification of each serials record loaded to date and arranged in Dewey call-number sequence; (ii) to produce a report for verification of each serials record loaded in the current run; and

(iii) to produce a report of any record or records containing erroneous information (errors, duplicated records).

Inputs to the system are: (i) a paper tape containing new serials records; and (ii) A paper tape containing corrections, additions, and deletions to be made in existing computer records.

Translate and Edit Programme of the System

It is pertinent to note that first requirement of the programme is to produce a report listing each error found in the editing procedure. Based on the editing report the data processing operator will correct the errors (as described previously) and will re-enter the corrections into the computer in a later run of the translate and edit programme.

The second requirement is to assemble the input data into proper format as developed for the master serials record. Master Serials Record, shows the layout of the computer record which consists of five sections. The first section of the record is fixed in length and contains the majority of the data characterizes as "basic identification and control data." The second section is fixed in length and contains the accounting data including a five-year historical record of the payment of each serial subscription. (A five-year average of the increase in serials cost should permit forecasting of serials budgets with a high degree of reliability.)

The third section of the master serials record, variable in length, contains bibliographical information on each title. This includes the official entry, all subject entries, selected added entries, title changes, and all notes. Each of these items is variable in length and each field, except the official entry field, may contain more than one entry. For example, there might be two or three subject entries for a particular title. The fourth section, variable in length, is the claiming and receipt section. This portion of the record is generated internally by the check-in programme at the time it forecasts the receipt of each issue of a title.

The fifth section, variable in length, contains the binding information, the greater portion of which is created by the check-in programme at the time the updated information is received by the computer. Inputs to the programme are (i) paper tape of new serials records; and (ii) paper tape of correction records.

Output of the programme are: (i) serials transactions file on magnetic tape containing the new titles that have been loaded during a given run plus corrections to previous titles that were loaded at an earlier date and (ii) the editing report indicating what errors the computer has found during the edit process. Functions of the programme are: (i) to read in the data from the paper-tape reader (since the codes that are produced by the paper-tape typewriter are not the same as the code structure used in the computer, the characters on this tape must be translated into the appropriate machine language); and (ii) to edit each field of the serials record to make sure that it conforms to the requirements of length and content of the field and that the information as presented is valid.

For example, under the area LIB (library) it is possible that the operator type a code that is not a valid departmental code—or in typing the MAIN ENTRY an invalid character was used or for an active serial the FREQ (frequency) code was omitted. Thus each item on the form, where it is possible, will be edited for validity and completeness.

Sort Programme of the System

The requirement of the programme is to sort the new serial record file into Dewey call-number sequence.

Input to the programme is the serials transactions file produced in the translate and edit programme and containing new and corrected serials records.

Output of the programme is a sorted serials transactions file containing new and corrected serials records in Dewey call-number sequence.

Function of the programme is to sort the records contained in the magnetic-tape files into a desired order or sequence.

Update Programme of the System

Requirements of the programme are: (i) to generate a new master serials record file; (ii) to make corrections to existing records; and (iii) to eliminate duplicate records.

Inputs to the programme are: (i) sorted serials transactions file of new and corrected serials record; and (ii) a sorted master file of existing serials records.

In fact, outputs of the programme are: (i) a magnetic tape file containing all records, existing and new, (ii) a printed listing of new and corrected titles loaded in this run, and (iii) a printed listing of erroneous records.

The main functions of the programme are: (i) to merge old and new records on the two input tapes into one output master file; and (ii) to correct any record in the old tape file prior to generating the new tape file.

Design of Computer Systems—Cartalog Report Generator System

The catalogue report generator system allows flexibility to the library staff and to the user by obtaining information from the system in the sequence and in the format wanted. This system is a medium by which users can exploit the informational potentialities of the serials control system.

Requirements of the system are: (i) to provide the user with an accurate and current catalogue of the serials holdings containing the necessary bibliographic information; and (ii) to provide the means whereby the user as well as staff members may request and receive special catalogs or reports of the serials holdings within a reasonable time.

Inputs to the system are: (i) the master magnetic tape file of serial records and (ii) the data control punched cards for selection of data and desired sequence and format of the report. Outputs of the system are printed catalogs or reports. When printout of these catalogs or reports is required, it is only necessary for the serials librarian to indicate this by the appropriate code in a control card.

The generator system based on this code will automatically select from the master record the data required for the printing of a given list.

Catalogue Report Generator of the System

The requirement of the programme is selection of desired information from the master file by means of the data control cards.

Inputs of the program are: (i) a the master file of serials records and (b) data control card for each item of information that is to appear in a given report.

The output of the programme is a magnetic-tape file containing information for each of the requested reports, or catalogs, or both.

Functions of the programme are: (i) stripping from the master serials record file the data required for the printing of catalogs or special reports as specified by the data control cards; and (ii) formatting such information and transferring the resulting record to an output work tape.

Sort Programme of the System

The requirement of this programme is to sort each of the report work tapes into desired sequence specified by the sort control card.

Inputs to the programme are: (i) the report work tapes created by the catalogue report generator programme; and (ii) the sort control cards that define the order in which records are to appear.

The output of the programme is a file of the records to be printed as a report or catalogue.

Utility Unit Programme of the System

The requirement of the programme is to print in desired format any standard catalogs or special reports.

Inputs to the programme are: (i) the sorted report file; and (ii) the print control card that defines the format in which the information is to appear. The output of the programme is the printed catalogue or report.

Operating Systems Design

In the preceding paragraphs, we have described in some detail the systems for compiling the original input to the serials system for setting up the master record file and for correcting this file and for setting up the reporting system required to produce the necessary reports or catalogs. The primary purpose of the serials operating systems is to provide efficient and accurate control of all records and the transactions.

Outline the programs and their interrelationships that are necessary to fulfill the following requirements:

1. Guarantee that all issues not received by the library will be claimed promptly and on a set schedule and that the renewal of all serials will be controlled by the system.

2. Predict the time of receipt of the journal thereby establishing a positive control over the timely receipt of all issues.
3. Maintain and control the accounting records necessary for the serials system internally as well as report to the comptroller the information required for payment of invoices.
4. Provide the binding department with the necessary information and records for those titles that are to be bound.
5. Handle the many changes that occur in the various serials titles.

Main outputs of the operating systems are: (i) an updated master file of all serials records; (ii) punched control cards anticipating receipt of issues; (iii) reports for controlling, claiming, renewals, and binding; and (iv) statistical and accounting reports.

Coming to periodicity, the operated systems work within three time frames: monthly, weekly, and daily. We shall now review functions that are performed by both the computer and the clerical.

Monthly Operating Functions

In fact monthly run of the check-in programme is the key to the successful fulfillment of the operating system. It is the function of this program to forecast the transactions that are to occur within the serials system for the coming month and to produce the reports and control cards that are needed to handle successfully these transactions.

The monthly run of the check-in programme has specific functions that must be performed.

1. A forecasting must be made of the issues to be

received for each of the active during the coming month. Utilizing the FREQ (frequency) data in conjunction with the months of publication data (JFM....field) the programme will determine whether an issue is to be received or claimed; the check-in programme will determine, when possible, the volume and issue numbers to received in the coming period. A control card will be punched for each issue to be received. Simultaneously the programme will post in the waiting receipt and claims section of the master record the control data for each particular issue. The check-in cards will be filed in the serials department awaiting receipt of the issue.

2. A listing must be produced of all titles whose subscriptions are to be renewed during the second month following the monthly run. (For example, during the June run the computer will forecast those titles to be renewed during August of that year.) This programme determines the renewal date by utilizing the date of last renewal found in the DATE SUBS START (date subscription start field and the period of the last subscription from the SUBS LGT (subscription length) field, both found in the accounting data section of the master record. The renewal report is produced by vendor or by publisher showing the titles that should be renewed in the period. The report contains the call number, the title, the last renewal date, the subscription length, and the estimated price of renewal. At this point, programme also produces a control card for each item being renewed. The control card contains the call number and short title. The programme also posts to the accounting data control section the renewal cost incurred.

3. A binding report is necessary for those titles with sufficient consecutive issues to warrant binding into a physical volume. A control card is produced for each volume to be bound

and an indication is made in the binding control section of the master record that an order has been issued for binding.

4. Accounting reports are required for the financial control of the system. These reports are based on encumbrances incurred by each fund and department account. In order to obtain a net balance for each fund and department account at the end of each month the encumbrances are adjusted to actual cost on receipt of invoices.

5. The programme must generate monthly statistics of the number of new titles added and their cost, the number of renewals and the estimated cost of renewals, the number of issues received, the number of bound volumes added to the serials collection, and other statistical information.

eVIDENTLY all titles frequency of receipt is irregular the check-in programme will, on the receipt of an issue, produce a check-in card for the next arrival. This card contains only the call number and the short title of the issue and, if possible, the volume and the issue number but not the month or year.

Daily Operating Functions

This section describes the function of the staff of the serials system and the data processing operator in maintaining records.

1. *Check-in:* When an issue is received, the serials clerk removes from the punched-card file the corresponding check-in card for the particular volume and issue. In the case of an irregular publication it is necessary to record on the check-in card (if not there already) the volume and issue number, adding the month and year of publication. The clerk marks the call number on the issue and checks for changes such as title and frequency in the journal.

If variations are not found, the check-in card and is forwarded to the data processing operator. If changes have occurred, they are recorded on the serials control record worksheet, indicating the call number and the changes in the appropriate fields.

The check-in card and the worksheet are forwarded to the data processing operator who, using the auxiliary punched-card reader attached to the paper-tape typewriter, enters the check-in card data into the paper tape. The call number, issue, month, and year are punched into the paper tape as input to the weekly run of the check-in programme. If corrections or changes to a given title are made, the data processing operator holds these until the end of the day or week when the correction tape for input to the translate and edit programme is produced.

2. *Renewal of Subscriptions:* The renewal control cards and the renewal reports are received from the computer. The renewal punched card is filed. The renewal report is verified and two copies forwarded to the supplier or the publisher for the renewal of the indicated titles. When the invoice, the invoice is received, the renewal control card for each title on the invoice, the invoice number, and the amount of the renewal are posted to the renewal control card. The renewal control report is checked for each title and the renewal control card is then forwarded to the data processing operator. The operator duplicates the prepunched information on the renewal control card and key punches the new information (invoice date and number and renewal cost) and simultaneously produces a punched paper tape with this information. This is accomplished by using a key punch that is cabled to the paper-tape typewriter.

3. *Ordering of New Serial Titles:* On receipt of the first

issue of a new title the serials librarian prepares a serials control record worksheet that is forwarded to the data processing operator for entry of the new title into the system.

4. *Claiming of Serial Issues:* The weekly run of the check-in programme prints out the claim notices. These notices are reviewed prior to mailing because notice may have been received from the supplier or publisher that item will be delayed. In such event the computer record is updated. If the claim is routine, the notice is forwarded to the supplier. On receipt of the claimed issue the check-in card for that issue is removed from the file and forwarded to the data processing operator.

5. *Binding Control:* On receipt of the binding control list and the control cards the binding department uses the control list as its worksheet for the coming month. The jour-nals are taken from the shelves and checked for completeness. Binding orders are then prepared for the completed volumes. It is the responsibility of the binding clerk to submit correction reports for any issues or indexes found missing.

At end of each week all input paper tapes for the serials system are forwarded to the computer center for entry into the weekly run of the check-in programme. These tapes are processed through the translate and edit programme. The output of this translate and edit programme. The output of this sort programme, arranged by call number and type of transaction, is the input to the weekly run of the check-in programme.

The function of the check-in programme is to post all transactions that have occurred to the serials master record file. The primary output of the weekly check-in programme is the claim notices.

During the weekly run the programme audits each record, comparing the date of a forecasted arrival in the WAITING RECEIPT sector of the record to the CLAIM CTL (claim control) date. If the issue is overdue, a claim is issued. If a subsequent published issue is received prior to the receipt of an earlier published issue, a claim is issued is received, the WAITING RECEIPT sector of the record is cleared and the issue is posted to the binding control section of the record.

The output of the weekly run is the updated serials master control file that is always the source of all printed reports.

Obviously, a critical operation within the serials system is the check-in and claiming of journal issues. There is an alternative to the punched card, paper-tape check-in and claiming operations in the computer-based serials system. The direct use of the punched from the check-in file as input to the weekly run of the check-in programme could be a more efficient way to update the master serials record file.

If the punched cards produced by the computer for the check-in operation contained the required information for check-in, the intermediate step of paper tape might well be eliminated. If this were done, no translate program would be necessary because punched cards do not require this.

This phase of the weekly programme would only require a card-to-tape utility programme. Another alternative could be that instead of punched cards, a monthly printout listing of expected journal issues could be used. After a journal issue is received, it could be crossed off the printed list, marked, and sent to the shelves.

At the end of the month the printout would be sent to the claiming subsystem for processing. Those titles not crossed off would require a claims notice. The initial notice, both to the vendor and the computer record, would be produced on the paper-tape typewriter. Subsequent claim notices would be issued by the claims programme under computer control.

Updating the computer record with information about the issues that have been received would be accomplished by the computer not being notified. If no notice were received, programming would provide for the computer record to be updated automatically on the assumption that the issue had been received.

The advantage, if any, of the printout listing over the 80-column punched-card record is mainly in the printout's not having to be concerned with abbreviated titles and other truncated bibliographic data.

Thus it becomes obvious from the preceding discussion that computer-based serials system is more convenient and practical than the traditional one. In the light of continuing developments there is much scope of improvement and functionality.

7

Effects of Technology on Library Staff

> "A famous author was presented with a copy of a book containing several anecdotes about himself. Who acknowledging the gift the wrote: 'I enjoyed immensely the stories about myself .... especially those I hadn't heard before.'"

As we know technology has come up in big way. Old practices in library and information science are changing very fast. We have to keep pace with them and should be ready for suitable adaptation.

In the present chapter we have made an attempt to portray the impact of technology on library professionals.

Changing Workload on Members of the Staff

Under upcoming conditions of modern hi-tech, it seems generally agreed in the library profession that technological applications have placed greater demands on members of the staff. Most obvious is the fact that they have had to learn to use various computer-based systems, and this requirement has become more onerous with the increase in number and diversity of the systems. For example, a reference librarian may now need to search databases accessible online through several different vendors, as well as some available in the library on CD-ROM, and this will require knowledge of different software and search capabilities.

For each of the overt demands associated with a particular technology, some more covert demands may also be created. For example, the librarian may have to instruct users in database searching techniques, which adds a new dimension to the requirement: a good searcher is not necessarily a good teacher.

It is significant to note that librarians involved in database searching must also be effective communicators since they need to interact with users to fully understand what it is they are looking for. While the ability to communicate has always been a requirement of public service librarians, the database searching situation enhances this requirement: in general, greater communication skills are needed in the database searching situation than in other aspects of reference service.

Moreover, effective database searching may also require more knowledge of the subject matter dealt with, especially its terminology, which implies a greater need for some level of subject specialization. Furthermore, some librarians now provide reference service to remote users who communicate with the library through electronic mail, and this presents a special challenge since it precludes the traditional face-to-face reference interview. There is another loss obvious requirement associated with this particular technology.

As well as knowing how to search databases, the librarian must have a good knowledge of the range of databases available in order to select the one most likely to satisfy a user request. This may in fact be the most stringent requirement associated with the growth of database searching. It is well illustrated by the case of the librarian of a small special library in industry who, thirty years ago, had only five or six databases available to search (printed indexing/abstracting services) but today has several hundred accessible through online networking. It is perhaps little wonder that librarians do not always select the database most appropriate but, instead, return frequently to the source or sources with which they are most familiar.

Obviously technology has increased demands on library staff in other ways. Automated systems require greater accuracy and rigor in use, due in part to the fact that more standardization is needed to facilitate intra-institutional and inter-institutional resource sharing. Moreover, automation exposes the individual's work to wider scrutiny.

The most obvious manifestation is the contribution of original cataloging to a large bibliographic utility, but other examples also exist since files that were once the exclusive domain of a particular department may now be accessed by all library staff members, and even, perhaps, by members of the public. Library users also place greater demands on the staff because they tend to expect more from the automated library than they did before. These heightened expectations range from better recordkeeping (e.g., users may expect the automated circulation system to indicate which books they have borrowed and they are due) to higher level of information service.

Stoffle et al. (1966) have put this situation clearly and provocatively :

> Despite the fact that libraries have over time conditioned their customers to expect little, faculty and students are less willing to accept slow or shoddy service or to accept personal responsibility for failure in getting what

they need. Expectations of traditional library service and response time have escalated, fueled by a culture of instant gratification.

Changing Skills

Here it must be noted that some of the new or enhanced skills implied by the automated library environment have already been alluded to. Others can also be recognized. For example, the librarian of toady may need to understand the principles of marketing in order to develop new user-responsive services and to promote them within the community.

In fact, staff members must now be more flexible and versatile since they are likely to engage in a greater variety of tasks than they did in the past. However, a somewhat anomalous situation has arisen; while they are expected to be more interchangeable, they may also be expected to develop more specialized skills—e.g., in database searching—and even to acquire a stronger background in a particular subject area. All of this suggests that the librarian of today needs to know more, and to possess a greater variety of skills, than the librarian of twenty or thirty years ago.

This has led to dissatisfaction among some staff members who feel that they now face greater pressures and responsibilities without a commensurate increase in status or financial reward.

It is significant to note that the librarian must now be more adaptable in another way. The library and the library profession are going through a period of considerable change. Indeed, electronic networks can radically alter one's ideas about what constitutes a "library" and what is involved in "librarianship." In this environment the librarian must be flexible in attitude of mindable to keep pace with and adapt to dramatic changes in the library itself and in the technological and social environments in which it operates. In the larger libraries, a split may occur between the staff members who enthusiastically embrace technology and those who do not. This can lead to resentment because the former, who may be younger and have less experience, might advance more rapidly in position and remuneration.

Professional/Nonprofessional Relationships

As mentioned in Chapter 2, automated systems allow some of the task formerly performed by professional librarians to be passed down to paraprofessionals, clerks, or, in some cases, library users themselves. This trend is well represented in the philosophy put forward by Gorman (1987):

1. no professional should do a task which can be performed by a paraprofessional;
2. no paraprofessional should do a task which can be performed by a clerical staff member;
3. no human being should do a task which can be performed by a machine. (Page 158).

Remarkably, some library tasks, such as the generation of over-due notices and notices of books being held for users, have been taken over by the computer, while others have actually been taken on by library users in some places—e.g., the charging out of books or the initiation of interlibrary lending activities. On the other hand, while some clerical tasks have been eliminated by automation, others, have emerged, including tasks associated with data input, the conversion of records, and system backup and maintenance activities.

At the same time, while professional librarians have

passed certain activities down to paraprofessionals, they have taken others on—in system development and implemen-tation, in learning system capabilities, in teaching, and in the design and operation of new services. In general, more of the professional functions of today occur in the public services arena rather than that of technical services.

Training Requirements

We know, automation has brought with it the need for more on-the-job training of staff and for the upgrading of their skills, especially when new technologies are introduced or significant changes are made to an existing system. Such training activities can be a major component of total automation costs—as much as fifty percent by some estimates. While some staff members will be eager to learn new skills and acquire additional experience, others may feel that too much of their time is spent in adapting to a changing technological environment, at the expense of direct service to the public, and that automation has brought about training overkill.

Creth (1995) points out how important it is for the manager to "develop a culture in which the process of continuous learning and an acceptance of change by staff is the norm."

Job Satisfaction and Self-Image

It seems widely accepted by within the library profession that automation has improved job satisfaction and the self-image of the professional librarian and other members of the library's staff. This is understandable: the professional librarians have relinquished some of the jobs they consider less important, while the paraprofessionals and clerical staff have also given up some of the most routine tasks (to the computer) and taken on others that are more satisfying and that they perceive as more "professional." One of the reasons why librarians have embraced technology with enthusiasm is the expectation that this will improve their image with library users and perhaps eventually increase their status within the communities served. Recent surveys of attitudes toward libraries and librarians suggest that no improvement of this kind has actually occurred.

Notably, a number of surveys have looked at the effects of automation on the attitudes of library workers towards their jobs. Among the more interesting is a study of attitudes among four groups in Australian academic libraries, as reported by Waters (1988). The results of Prince and Burton (1988) are more positive but show that major difference may exist from one library to another. While 45% of the staff in one British academic library report that their jobs are now more interesting (50% report no change), only 33% do so in a second library (67% no change) and 23% in a third. In the last case, 31% report that the work has become less interesting.

As such, based on an emperical survey in three libraries in the United States, Jones (1989) reports that support staff (paraprofessional and clerical) are generally positive toward technology. In fact, many of the more than one hundred respondents feel that automation has been introduced too slowly. However, she reports overwhelming agreement that the support staff should have greater involvement in decisions made on the acquisition of new systems or capabilities.

Edwards et al. (1955), used questionnaires, interviews and other sources to study attitudes of staff in six academic libraries in the United Kingdom. While many support staff felt that "electronic information" had reduced their workload, the majority of professional librarians disagreed, although all groups reported increase in job satisfaction and that they felt more effective in their work.

The majority, professional librarians and support staff alike, find it difficult to keep up with new developments and are frustrated by their "lack of technical expertise." There was strong agreement that technology does not foster isolation—either from library users of others staff members—and that it is unlikely to lead to loss of jobs.

A somewhat surprising finding is that, while respondents are enthusiastic about working with electronic tools, they seem to feel little confidence in them.

It is sometimes claimed that the librarian of today must be more extrovert than the librarian of yesterday. The implication behind this claim is that the librarian now spends more time in direct contact with library users. There is some justification for this belief in the sense that more professional hours are now devoted to public services, rather than the behind-the-scenes technical services, than was true in the past.

Nevertheless, the fact that librarians now spend more time being trained and in committee or task force meetings, coupled with the fact that paraprofessionals may now provide more of the public service functions, or library users perform them for themselves, suggests that hours of direct contact between professional librarians and the public may actually have declined. In some libraries, contact between users and nonprofessional members of the staff may also have declined as users take on more activities for themselves. At least, a decline in contact with the public may be a perception of many nonprofessionals, who may feel that the library, as a result, has become a less congenial working environment.

Not all librarians are of the belief that technology will improve their image and status. Harris (1992) points out that improvements in the ability of librarians to exploit technology may have caused a deterioration in others expertise. She is supported in this by those reference librarians who complain that the amount of time they now spend with electronic resources threatens their familiarity with the printed sources.

Drawing upon the work of sociologist Toren (1975), Harris claims that deprofessionalization occurs when a profession loses control over its knowledge base and service ideal. Lancaster (1991, 1993b) has suggested that the profession may well be losing its service idea because he believes that many librarians have become mesmerized by the glamour of technology, seeing automation as an end in rather than a means of improving range, scope, and quality of services. Harris (1992), on the other hand, sees the profession losing control over its knowledge base. Skilled professional catalogers have been replaced by network copy cataloging and, she believes, end user searching of CD-ROM and other databases will mean less demand for the services of search specialist.

Harris contends that

> ...the loss of the service ideal and loss of control over a knowledge base through the routinizing of professional functions, will lead to deprofessionalization. In other words, the changes underway in librarianship are likely to lead to its demise as a profession. (Page 14)

It is remarkable here that a debate held at the 1995 annual meeting of the Medical library Association posed various questions of library administrators that do reflect concerns relating to the staff morale, loss of the service deal, and possible transfer of tasks to other types of professionals.

Among these questions, focused specifically on reference services, were the following :

(a) Is a "reference librarian" needed to develop and provide instruction for electronic resources? Can't systems staff do this better?

(b) How do you maintain staff moral in a constantly changing environment, where responsibilities are fluid, additional services are added, and staff are reduced?

(c) How do we bring other staff (nonlibrarians) into sour reference/teaching activities and still keep clear lines among responsibilities, rewards, position levels, etc.? Or, do we want to have those lines?....

(d) Are public services librarians losing their commitment to user service? Are they becoming overly fascinated and involved with the electronic world and forgetting how to apply it to their specific users' needs?

(e) How is service to users affected when reference desk hours are shortened so that staff can have more time to evaluate new electronic resources and develop print and on-screen guides for users? (Nagle, 1996).

Employee Dichotomy

In some cases the fear is of the technology itself, and its possible effects, such as the fear that books will be replaced.

In fact, Fine (1986) has pointed out that about twenty percent of the members of the staff may be resistant to technology even today. Much of this resistance stems from fear, which may be associated with the introduction of a new system or with changes in an existing system.

A second feat is that of making a mistake that will damage the equipment, wipe out a file, or otherwise prove costly to the organization. Older employees in particular may be afraid that they will be unable to learn how to use a new system. There may well be some justification for this because organizations rarely have enough resources to train all staff members adequately, especially in a situation in which the system is in a period of rapid change. Some employees may fear that their jobs are threatened although, as already discussed, automation in libraries had led to redeployment of staff and changing responsibilities rather than actual staff reductions.

A related fear, also touched upon earlier, is that of deprofessinalization and the loss of traditional skills (e.g., the fear that print-related skills will decline as more reference work involves use of electronic resources).

Other fears relate to reduced socialization—if tied to a terminal for a large part of the day, one will have less contact with other staff members or with the public—and to the Big Brother phenomenon (is the computer spying on me?). Finally, there may exist far of possible health hazards. While extreme cases may reflect simple paranoia, some justification exists for concerns relating to less serious effects such as backache and eyestrain.

Remarkably fears are best handled by giving employees greater involvement with the technology through demonstrations, workshops, and visits to institutions in which the technology to be introduced is already in place. Most fears are best handled by giving employees greater involvement with the technology through demonstrations, workshops, and visits to institutions in which the technology to be introduced is already in place. Resistance to technology can take various forms (see, for example, Fine, 1986): decline in quality or quality or work, unwillingness to change or to learn, absenteeism or lateness, behavioral problems (apathy, boredom, negativism, withdrawal or even aggression), and, in extreme cases, physiological problems such as headache, nausea or high blood pressure.

Olsgaard (1985) has identified the factors that determine whether or not technology is introduced successfully into an organization. The problem occur in a logical progression from those that are purely technological to those that are behavioral. First, and most obviously, the system adopted must be effective in doing what it is supposed to do. Second, the transition of the new system must be well planned and the staff well trained.

The management must be strongly committed to the system and able to convey the strength of this commitment throughout the organization. Finally, management must work to minimize conflict among individuals or departments—related, for example, to changing responsibilities and organizational structure—and to minimize the effects of resistance in those individuals opposed to the change.

It is apt here to quote Jackson (1993a) who says that the addition of a new technology, if it is to be well accepted,

> ...must be carefully planned and integrated into existing procedures. If not it will probably be relegated to infrequent use or used only in extreme rush situations.

In fact, she was referring specifically to new document delivery systems but the principle applies equally to other technologies. Fine (1986) suggests that it may be a good thing that some employees resist technology. The manager should not necessarily dismiss such people as mere problems. Sometimes those who resist have been able to see undesirable consequences of a proposed change that others have completely overlooked. She feels that healthy growth in an organization can result from the tension that exists those pulling for technology and those resisting.

Olsgaard (1985) points to the fact that there exists two opposing views on the behavioral effects of technology :

1. The more experience one has with technology, the more positive one is about its capabilities.
2. The more one uses the technology, the more aware one is its limitations and dangers.

While most librarians seem to fall into the first group, this situation may be changing. The introduction of computers into libraries at a significance level, in the 1970's, was met with hostility, skepticism or indifference among many members of the profession.

This eventually gave way to somewhat pervasive overenthusiasm and overoptimism regarding the benefits of technology. While this still exists to a very large extent, it is encouraging to find that some librarians are now more realistic in judging the effects of technology. Recently, for example, Ewing and Hauptman (1955) and LaGaurdia (1955) imply that reference librarians at least may have lost more than they have gained.

Ewing and Hauptman put it this way:

> ...technologies incorporated into libraries to economize or to make access easier have rarely done either, what they have done is to transmute the reference librarian's ostensible intellectual endeavors into manual tasks. Microformat readers and printers, photocopiers, desktop computers and workstations, and associated printers, output devices, CD-ROM drives, and debit card systems all require varying degrees of maintenance, [and] repair, and often demand immediate assistance and/or instruction.

Simultaneously, LaGuardia believes that the major problem is a different one. To quote her

> The truth is, technology has not yet delivered on all its promises to us. Instead of saving our patrons and us time, it demands more and more of us. The logistical stuff, paper jams, ink cartridge replacements, and CD-ROM swapouts consume time at a reference desk, but they are still small consideration in comparison to the systems that are requiring major investments of time and effort to learn and pass on to our users, either at the desk or in library classes. We find ourselves working full-tilt just to keep up with the basic tools we need to know. We cannot access everything that is now available to us via networks and in print, but we are complicit with others in the information industry in creating a new myth; the myth that we *can* do it all, under present operating conditions.

On the other hand, based on "in-depth interviews" with librarians from several universities, Tenopir and Neufang (1992) claim that the majority feel that reference work is now more exciting and rewarding, so it is obvious that significant differences of opinion still exist on the impact of technology on the profession.

It is obvious from the above discussion that every

library professional of present times must equip themselves with latest technological knowledge. Many amazing gifts of science and technology are upcoming. We should welcome these and ready for adaptation.

8

Challenge of Information Materials Preparation

> "Such help as we can give each others in this world is a debt to each other; and the man who perceives a superiority or a capacity in a subordinate, and neither confesses nor assists it, is not merely the withholder of kindness, but the committer of injury."
>
> —***John Ruskin***

Among library systems acquisition of library materials is important. A library professional should know very well how the library collections are prepared.

Here in the present chapter we will acquaint you with publishing of library materials.

First, it is worth mentioning that producers of information materials are grappling with technology issues just as are libraries. First, in the opening paragraph about the Booker Prize, the question of what *is* a book was raised; second, later in the chapter, the issue of how to handle pricing of electronic materials was introduced. Richard Cox addressed some of the issues in his article "Taking Sides on the Future of the Book", in which he commented on the Internet, books-on-demand, electronic books and other nonprint/nonlinear electronic resources. Those words are probably reasonable descriptors of the behavior of a great many of us and, in our opinion, will remain so for some time to come. They are also probably good indicators for what a great many producers of information materials are and will be doing for some time: producing a mix of traditional and electronic products.

In the past, one could categorize information producers by product: (1) those who produced printed matter (books, periodicals, newspapers and the like) and (2) those who produced audiovisual materials. Seldom did a producer work in both areas. Today the situation is different. Though some companies are solely devoted to the production of print or audiovisual materials, most trade book publishers also have one or more electronic and audiovisual lines. University presses and other scholarly publishers are also moving into electronic publishing.

Writers have been predicting a paperless society, office, or library for some time. Despite such predictions, printed materials are still very much with us and probably will be for some time. Print materials still comprise the largest percentage of items available through most libraries and information centers. Some sense of the staying power of print is found in sources such as *Books in Print (RIP)*. The 1988 edition of *RIP* listed 781,292 titles; by 1998 that number had more than doubled to over 1.6 million. Certainly electronic products are being produced, but as of 1999 they had not noticeably slowed the production of print materials. A major reason for the staying power of books is that paper copies still provide the least expensive means of distributing large quantities of timely information to a large number of people. Certainly one can mount a long document (300 or more pages) on the Internet; many people do. Further, it is obvious that any number of individuals can simultaneously read that document.

However, very few individuals using that material attempt to read it off the computer screen. Rather, they print some portion or the entire file and read the material in a printed form. (Anyone with experience in a reference department is well aware of the volume of printing being done of electronic data, most of which is in relatively short files).

Also, some people are uncomfortable with technology-based information sources.

There is always some question, with electronic files, about the integrity of the material: is what one sees on the screen what the author originally input? Finally, many people still like to read in bed, on the subway, at the beach and other places where technology-based systems are inconvenient, if not impossible, to use. (Try reading a CRT screen in full sunlight at the beach).

The first portion of this chapter examines publishing, that is, the production of printed material, with comments about the changing nature of the field. The second portion discusses audiovisual production. (The chapters on serials, government documents, Web resources and electronic materials, as well as others, all touch on issues related to the electronic information environment of today). The chapter provides an overview of the important production characteristics of both types of products, with enough depth for one to begin to understand how information producers operate.

What is publishing? That question has been with us, at least in the United States, for almost 300 years. Publishers and others have debated whether publishing's purpose was/is cultural or commercial, or both.

In the abstract and to some degree in the real world, "the book" is a cultural artifact as well as an essential means of recording and preserving the culture of a society. Certainly libraries of all types have, to a greater or lesser degree, some role to play in preserving and passing on their society's cultural values and heritage. Thus, books have taken on a special aura of importance—some might even say sacredness—that is very different from that of, say, clothes, cars, or cameras. Discarding worn-out items like the latter may bring some scowls from a few people. However, there is widespread disapproval of doing the same with a book.

From early childhood one hears, "don't bend the pages", "wash your hands before using your books", "treat your books with respect"—and being labelled a "book burner" is something no one wants. Because of the cultural and literary aspects involved in the production of books, there is some sense that a literate society *must* have a publishing program of some type. Further, that publishing *must* produce books for the good of society. Sometimes supporters of the cultural purpose seem to paint a picture of noble people—from writer, to editor, to owner—who are free of the concerns of economics and profit. Does that mean, then, that there should be no concern with costs? Clearly not. The romantic view of publishing is nice but unrealistic; even most government publications have a price.

The fact is, the bottom line of publishing is the bottom line. Without an expectation of a reasonable return, why would anyone invest time and money in publishing? Certainly one can debate what "reasonable" means, but no one should question the need for a return beyond that of survival. The return ought to be greater than that of putting the money in an insured savings account, as there are substantial risks in publishing—not everything sells as fast as one might hope, if it sells at all. Publishers are in the commercial world and often they have stockholders to take into account as well as the interests of readers and society.

It is apt to quote here Albert Greco, who says:

> Many industry analysts believe that publishing is in disarray, dangerously weakened by steep returns, stark sales figures, fickle and price sensitive customer base, the "rise" of chains and super-stores and price clubs and the concomitant "decline" of independent book store[s], a population more interested in watching television than in reading books, paper thin profit margins, staggering technological challenges and author advances that dumbfound even seasoned industry veterans .... Its best days are indeed ahead, a fact that excites tens of thousands of people every day about this wonderful, funny and, at times, hard business.

Practically, publishing is both a cultural and a commercial activity, but without the commercial there would be no cultural purpose. Librarians should be among the first to discard the stereotype of the publisher as a retiring, highly sophisticated literary person interested only in creative quality, just as publishers should abandon the view of the librarian as a woman with her hair in a bun, wearing horn-rimmed glasses, with a constant "shush" on her lips. When one is going to work day in and day out with an industry, even if one is just buying its products, some knowledge of that industry will make everyone's life a little easier. An understanding of the trade's characteristics—such as how producers determine prices, how they distribute products and what services one can expect—can improve communication between producers and buyers.

Under the best of circumstances, a great deal of communication exists between the library and the trade regarding orders. This knowledge provides the librarian with some understanding of, if not sympathy for, the problems of producers. Publishers who depend on library sales know (or should know) a great deal about library problems and operations. They often joke about how uninformed librarians are about the trade. The present strained relationship between libraries and publishers developed, in part, because neither group fully understood nor tried to understand the other's position. Yet, we also know that when two parties discuss problems with mutual understanding of the other's position,. the working relationship will be more pleasant.

Each is more willing to make an occasional concession to the others needs; this flexibility can, in turn, foster mutually beneficial alliances. Book selection and collection development courses in library schools usually touch only lightly on publishers and their problems, as teachers often claim there is insufficient time to give more coverage to this important topic. Further, courses in the history of the book trade seldom have time to deal with the contemporary situation, because it is not yet history.

Most schools' curricula do not have a place for a course in contemporary production. Even if they did, most students would not have time for it in their one-year course of study. For this reason, students lack information that could prove invaluable, because knowing what happens in publishing can affect the selection process. First, knowing something about publishing helps selectors identify the most likely sources of materials; that is, which among the thousands of producers are most likely to produce the needed material. Second, by keeping up-to-date with what is happening in publishing, one can anticipate changes in quality and format.

Third, librarians may be able to influence publishing decisions, if the publisher is aware that the librarian is knowledgeable about the issues involved in developing profitable books.

Publishers supply the capital and editorial assistance required to transform an author's manuscript into books and electronic products. Generally, publishers in Western countries perform six basic functions:

1. Tap sources of materials (manuscripts).
2. Raise and supply the capital to make the books.
3. Aid in the development of the manuscript.
4. Contract for the manufacturing (printing and binding) of books.
5. Distribute books, including promotion and advertising.
6. Maintain records of sales, contracts and correspondence relating to the production and sale of books.

A thumbnail sketch of the basic publishing development pattern is pertinent. The pattern seems to be worldwide and it does have an impact on acquisition and selection work. In the history of publishing, there appear to be three stages of development. These stages have occurred in both Europe and America. They also appear elsewhere in the world.

In stage one, the publishing, printing and selling of the product are all combined into one firm. The early giants of printing in Europe acted as publisher, printer and retail bookseller. These publishers included Froben, Schoffer, Manutius, Caxton and others. When one examines American publishing history, the same pattern appears on the eastern seaboard and moves west with the frontier; names like Franklin, Green and Harris crop up during this period.

Elsewhere in the world, publishing exhibits a similar evolutionary pattern, which is largely a function of how societies organize economic, educational and human resources. In countries with limited resources, technical skills and small markets, it is unfeasible and in many cases impossible, to have specialty publishers in all fields. From a collection development point of view, a publishing industry in stage one presents many interesting challenges. Research libraries buy materials from around the world, but countries with weak economies and low literacy rates seldom have anything resembling a national bibliography or trade bibliography (mainstays in identifying important titles).

As if this were not enough of a challenge, most publishers operating at this level print a limited number of copies of each book. In many cases, they take orders before printing the book. When they do this, they print just a few more copies than the number ordered. Many collection development officers have experienced the frustration of having an order returned with the comment "unavailable, only 200 copies printed". Some books are, in fact, out of print on the date of publication; this frequently occurs in areas where publishing is at the stage-one level. In stage two, specialization begins, with firms emphasizing publishing or printing. New firms, many with a single emphasis, appear. The factors creating this situation relate to available economic, educational and human resources. Better education creates a greater market for books among both individual and institutional buyers. The retail trade develops at the same time, because the reading public exists countrywide and a single outlet in the country's major population center is no longer adequate.

Publishers from this period in American publishing history include John Wiley, George Putnam and the Lippincott Company. In 1807, Charles Wiley joined George Putnam in a bookstore operation in New York City. During the following 150 years, the heirs of the two men built two of the leading publishing houses in the United States. The Lippincott Company started in 1836 as a bookstore; over the years it shifted its emphasis to publishing. Often, when bookstores begin to develop, a company will decide to create a listing or publication through which publishers inform bookstores about new and existing titles. Collection development librarians expend time and energy trying to track down such systems in countries where the book trade is in stage two. The usual procedure is to establish a good working relationship with a large bookstore, with that shop functioning as a purchasing agent. This may entail signing an agreement to spend a certain amount of money each year with the store, but it normally results in much better coverage and usually better service, than trying to buy directly from the publishing houses.

The third stage is the complete separation of the three basic functions, as publishers discontinue printing activities. For example, John and James Harper started as printers in 1817. Today, Harper Collins is one of the leading publishers in the United States. It ceased printing years ago.

Two of the last major publishers to retain printing

plants are McGraw-Hill and Doubleday. When publishing reaches stage three, all the trappings we see in contemporary U.S. Publishing are evident: specialty publishers, literary agents, trade journals, sales personnel, jobbers and wholesalers and so forth. Normally, there is something resembling a national bibliography as well as a trade bibliography, both of which are essential for collection development work. Canadian, U.S. and European publishers have undergone two other changes since reaching the third level of development in publishing. Before 1950, most publishing houses existed as family-owned or privately held firms. With the rapid expansion of the educational market, especially in the United States, most publishers found it impossible to raise enough capital to expand adequately. Slowly at first and then with increasing frequency, publishers sold stock in the firm to the public. Going public generated several changes in the publishing field, some good and some bad.

On the positive side, publishers issued more new material and offered more services. On the negative side, publicly held companies placed an increased emphasis on profitability, with, perhaps, a decline in overall quality. The problems were neither as great nor as bad as the doomsday prophets predicted. As governments spent more and more money on education in the late 1950s and early 1960s, educational publishing became increasingly profitable. High profitability made publishing an area of interest for large conglomerates looking for diversification, so large electronics and communication firms began to buy publishing houses.

The 1980s were known as a time of "merger mania" in the publishing industry; in the 1990s mergers continued, albeit at a somewhat slower rate. Two dated but relevant articles about mergers are Celeste West's "Stalking the Literary-Industrial Complex" and "The Question of Size in the Book Industry. Another older, but still valid, article that covers all media is Ben Bagdikian's "The Media Brokers". A more recent and balanced, assessment of mergers is chapter 3 in Albert Greco's 1997 work *The Book Publishing Industry* (Allyn & Bacon). According to one study, in 1987 the top 12 U.S. publishing houses accounted for 56 percent of all domestic and international publishing sales. The data covered all distribution channels: trade, mass-market, school textbook (elementary through high school, also called el-hi) and so forth. In the mid-1990s, if one could get accurate data, the results would probably be much the same.

Notably, late in 1998, Bertelsmann, a German media conglomerate, announced plans to buy Barnes & Noble's online division for $200 million. Barnes & Noble, in turn, raised eyebrows in late 1998 when it announced plans to invest in Ingram Book Group, at the time the nation's leading wholesale book distributor. Thus, the merger interest is still present in the late 1990s. The potential effect of these new combinations is great. If nothing else, it will mean that market potential will take on even greater importance when publishers select manuscripts to publish. Anyone with a little imagination can envision a future publishing industry that controls what the public may know. To date, little evidence indicates any real change in the quality of books being produced.

However, the threat of too few information producers with access to a free market still exists. Selection and acquisition librarians, if they are aware of what is happening in the publishing field and of the implications of changes, should be among the first to note any significant changes.

A fourth stage—electronic publishing—is quickly developing. Some publishers offer information in two or more formats (for example, print and electronic) and others offer some information only in an electronic format. For example, in 1992 Random House entered into a joint venture with Voyager Company (software) and Apple Computer. The group publishes both electronic and paper versions of Random House's Modern Library series. The group projects press runs of 7,500 to 15,000 books and 500 to 5,000 discs. Digital devices are creating a variety of opportunities for publishers. In a sense, the devices are almost as revolutionary as the introduction of movable type. Digitization is especially useful in the production process; submission of electronic manuscripts containing digitized images also speeds editorial work.

The implications of electronic publishing for the bottom line are clear to most publishers, as suggested by Gayle Feldman: "Whether it be CD-ROM opportunities for scholarly presses, document delivery revenue for journal publishers, or multimedia packages for the reference crowd ... the coffee breaks buzzed with conviction that publishers who ignore new technology do so at their peril". With the beginning of new millennium, few publishers are risking being left behind in a print-only world. Insight into the impact of technology on the published bottom line appeared in a *Publishers Weekly* (PW) report showing that a completely digital publisher spends an average of $ 13.60 per page to prepare material for printing. A traditional approach costs slightly over $43 per page.

Now about types of publishers. *Trade publishers* produce a wide range of titles, both fiction and nonfiction, that have wide sales potential. HarperCollins; Alfred A. Knopf; Doubleday; Macmillan; Little, Brown; Thames & Hudson;

and Random House are typical trade publishers. Many trade publishers have divisions that produce specialty titles, such as children's, college textbooks, paperback, reference and so forth. Trade publishers have three markets: bookstores, libraries and wholesalers.

To sell their products, publishers send sales representatives to visit buyers in businesses or institutions in each of the markets. *Specialty publishers* restrict output to a few areas or subjects. Gale Research is an example of a specialty publisher. Specialty publishers' audiences are smaller and more critical than trade publishers' audiences. The categories of specialty publishers include reference, paperback, children's, microform, music, cartographic and subject area. *Textbook publishers,* especially those that target the primary and secondary schools (el-hi), occupy one of the highest-risk areas of publishing. Most publishers in this area develop a line of textbooks for several grades, for example, a social studies series. Preparation of such texts requires large amounts of time, energy and money. Printing costs are high because most school texts feature expensive color plates and other specialized presswork. Such projects require large upfront investments that must be recouped before a profit can be realized.

If enough school districts adopt a text, profits can be substantial, but failure to secure adoption can mean tremendous loss. Larger textbook firms, such as Gina or Scott, Foresman, & Company, produce several series to help ensure a profit or to cushion against loss. Why would a company take the risk this type of publishing involves? Consider the amount of money spent on textbooks each year: more than $2.345 billion in 1995. Because of the scheduling practices in school textbook adoption (usually occurring once a year), textbook publishers can reduce warehousing costs, thus adding to the margin of profit.

During the 1990s U.S. El-hi publishers faced increased pressure to change the content of their publications from a variety of special-interest groups. This pressure adds yet another element of risk to textbook publishing. *Subject specialty* publishers share some of the characteristics of textbook houses. Many have narrow markets that are easy to identify. Focusing marketing efforts on a limited number of buyers allows specialty publishers to achieve a reasonable return with less risk than a trade publisher takes on a nonfiction title. Specialty houses exist for a variety of fields; examples include art (Harry N. Abrams), music (E. C. Schirmer), scientific (Academic Press), technical (American Technical Publishers), law (West Publishing) and medical (W. B. Saunders).

Many specialty books require expensive graphic preparation or presswork. Such presswork increases production costs, which is one of the reasons art, music and science and technology titles are so costly.

Another factor in their cost is the smaller market as compared to the market for a trade title. A smaller market means that the publisher must recover production costs from fewer books. Although the risk level is greater for specialty publishing than for trade publishing, it is much lower than that of el-hi publishers. *Vanity presses* differ from other publishing houses in that they receive most of their operating funds from the authors whose works they publish. An example is Exposition Press. Vanity presses always show a profit and never lack material to produce. They offer editing assistance for a fee and they arrange to print as many copies of the book as the author can afford.

Distribution is the author's chore. Although such presses provide many of the same functions as other publishers, they do not share the same risks.

Many authors who use vanity presses give copies of their books to local libraries, but such gifts usually arrive with no indication that they are gifts. Books arriving in the acquisitions department without packing slips or invoices cause problems. By knowing local publishers, persons in the acquisitions department can make their work easier. *Private presses* are not business operations in the sense that the owners expect to make money. Most private presses are an avocation rather than a vocation for the owners. Examples are Henry Morris, Bird and Poull Press. In many instances, the owners do not sell their products, but give them away instead. Most private presses are owned by individuals who enjoy fine printing and experimenting with type fonts and design. As one might expect, when the owner gives away the end product (often produced on a hand press), only a few copies are printed.

In the past, many developments in type and book design originated with private presses. Some of the most beautiful examples of typographic and book design originated at private presses. Thus, large research libraries often attempt to secure copies of items produced by private presses. *Scholarly publishers,* as part of not-for-profit organizations, receive subsidies. Most are part of an academic institution (University of California Press), museum (Museum of the American Indian Heye Foundation), research institution (Battelle Memorial Institute), or learned society (American Philosophical Society). Scholars established these presses to produce scholarly books that would not be acceptable to most for-profit publishers. Most scholarly books have limited sales appeal.

A commercial, or for-profit, publisher considering a scholarly manuscript has three choices: (1) publish it and try to sell it at a price that ensures cost recovery; (2) publish it, sell it at a price comparable to commercial titles and lose money; or (3) do not publish the item. Because of economic factors and a need to disseminate scholarly information regardless of cost (that is, even if it will lose money) the subsidized (by tax exemption, if nothing else), not-for-profit press exists. As publishing costs have skyrocketed, it has been necessary to fully subsidize some scholarly books, almost in the manner of a vanity press. The role of the scholarly press in the economical and open dissemination of knowledge is critical. Every country needs some form of this type of press. Without scholarly presses, important works with limited appeal do not get published. Certainly, there are times when a commercial house publishes a book that will not show a profit simply because the publisher thinks the book is important, but relying on that type of willingness, in the long run, means that many important works will never appear in print.

Further, *Government presses* are the world's largest publishers. The combined annual output of government publications—international (UNESCO), national (U.S. Government Printing Office) and state, regional and local (Los Angeles or State of California)—dwarfs commercial output. In the past, many people thought of government publications as characterized by poor physical quality or as uninteresting items that governments gave away. Today, some government publications rival the best offerings of commercial publishers and cost much less. (The government price does not fully recover production costs, so the price can be lower).

Most government publishing activity goes well beyond

the printing of legislative hearings or actions and occasional executive materials. Often, national governments publish essential and inexpensive (frequently free) materials on nutrition, farming, building trades, travel and many other topics. *Paperback publishers* produce two types of work: quality trade paperbacks and mass-market paperbacks. A trade publisher may have a quality paperback division or may issue the paperbound version of a book through the same division that issued the hardcover edition. The publisher may publish original paperbacks, that is, a first edition in paperback.

Distribution of quality paperbacks is the same as for hardcover books. Mass-market paperback publishers issue only reprints, or publications that first appeared in hardcover. Their distribution differs from other book distribution. Their low price is based, in part, on the concept of mass sales. Therefore, they sell anywhere the publisher can get someone to handle them.

The paperback books on sale in train and bus stations, airline terminals, corner stores and kiosks are mass-market paperbacks. These books have a short shelf life compared to hard-covers. People talk about the paperback revolution, but it is hard to think of it as a revolution. Certainly the paperback has affected publishers' and a few authors' incomes. Also, some readers are unwilling to accept a hardcover when the smaller, more compact paperback is more convenient for use. The low price of a paperback also appeals to book buyers. Books with paper covers are not new. In some countries all books come out with paper covers and buyers must bind the books they wish to keep. The major difference is that most people think of only mass-market paperbacks as paperbacks. The emphasis on popular, previously published titles issued in new and colorful covers and sold at a low price is apparent. Those are the elements of the paperback revolution, not the paper cover nor even the relatively compact form. Nor has the paperback created a whole new group of readers, as some overenthusiastic writers claim. It has merely tapped an existing market for low-cost, popular books.

Further a category, *Newspaper and periodical publishers* are a different class of publisher. Usually, book publishers depend on persons outside their organization to prepare the material that they publish. Newspaper and periodical publishers retain reporters or writers as members of their staffs. Of course, there are exceptions to the exception. For instance, some popular (and most scholarly) periodicals consist of articles written by persons not employed by the organization that publishes the journal. In general, in newspaper or periodical publishing, one finds the same range of activities found in book publishing.

In other words, there are commercial publishers of popular materials, specialty publishers, children's publishers, scholarly or academic publishers and government publishers. All subcategories share the characteristics of their book publishing counterparts; some are divisions of book publishing organizations. Supplying current information is the primary objective of newspaper and journal publishers. With books, one can assume that most of the material published is at least six months old at the time of publication.

The newspaper or periodical format provides the means for more rapid publishing, from two or three months to less than one day. (A major exception are some scholarly and academic periodicals, which frequently are one, two, or more years behind in publishing accepted articles). To provide the most current information available, the library must acquire the newspapers or periodicals that suit the community's needs and interests.

Two other types of publishing activities deserve mention: *associations* and *reprint houses.* Professional and special-interest groups and associations frequently establish their own publishing houses. The American Library Association is one such organization. These organizations may publish only a professional journal, but they also may issue books and audiovisual materials. The operating funds come from the association, but the association hopes to recover its costs. Professional associations are often tax-exempt and thus their publishing activities are similar to those of scholarly presses: limited-appeal titles, small press runs, relatively high prices and indirect government subsidies.

Some associations do not have paid publication staff and use volunteer members instead; they contract with a commercial publisher to print the group's journal, conference proceedings and other publications. Association publications, whether published by the organization itself or by contract, can provide the library with numerous bibliographic control headaches. For example, they announce titles as forthcoming, but the items never get published. Many publications are papers from meetings and conventions (called "Transactions of..." or "Proceedings of..."); the titles of such publications frequently change two or three times before they appear in hardcover. Many of these publications do not find their way into trade bibliographies. *Reprint* publishers, as the name implies, focus on reprinting items no longer in print. Most of the sales by reprint houses are to libraries and scholars and many of the titles that these publishers reprint are in the public domain (that is, no longer covered by copyright). The other major source of reprinted material is the purchase of rights to an out-of-print title from another publisher. Although many of the basic costs of creating a book do not exist for the reprint house (editing, design and royalties, for example), reprints are expensive because of their limited sales appeal. Sometimes reprints cause as many or more bibliographic headaches for libraries than do association titles. Despite the many problems, reprint houses are an essential source of titles for collection development programs concerned with retrospective materials. *Small presses* are important for some libraries. Small presses are thought of as literary presses by some people, including librarians. Anyone reading the annual "Small Press Round-Up" in *Library Journal* could reasonably reach the same conclusion. The reality is that small presses are as diverse as the international publishing conglomerates. Size is the only real difference; in functions and interests small presses are no different from large trade publishers.

Another factor that sets small presses apart from their larger counterparts is economics. Large publishers have high costs and need substantial sales to recover their costs, but small presses can produce a book for a limited market at a reasonable cost and still expect some profit. Small presses also can produce books more quickly than their larger counterparts. From a collection development point of view, small presses represent a challenge. Tracking down new releases can present a variety of problems. Locating a correct current address is one common problem. Another is learning about the title before it goes out of print.

With *SPRBIP,* Len Fulton of Dustbooks tries to provide access and he has succeeded to a surprising degree, given the nature of the field. However, waiting for his annual *SPRBIP* may take too long, because small presses frequently move about and their press runs are small (that is, only a limited quantity of books is printed). In essence, few small presses are part of the organized trade or national bibliographic network. Very few of these presses advertise and even fewer of their titles receive reviews in national journals. There are two publications that focus on small press titles, *Small Press Review* and *Small Press Book Review.* Lack of reviews is not the result of book review editors discriminating against small press publications.

Rather, it is a function of too many small press operators not understanding how items get reviewed and failing to send out review copies.

Collection development librarians interested in small presses have had some commercial help. Quality Books of Northbrook, Illinois (a vendor that in the past was known primarily as a source of remainder books), has become active in the distribution of small press publications. Although it stocks books from only a small percentage of the presses listed in *SPRBIP* (about one-fifth), the fact that it does stock the items is a major feature. Most jobbers say they will attempt to secure a specific title for a library if they do not stock the publication. A librarian could easily devote too much time to an effort to track down a single copy of a $10.95 item from an obscure small press.

Librarians interested in small presses, collection development and access to information need to keep their collective fingers crossed in the hope that Quality Books will find its operation sufficiently profitable and that it will continue to offer the service.

Publishing consists of five basic functions, which apply equally to print and nonprint materials: administration, editorial, production, marketing and fulfillment. A publisher must be successful in all five areas if the organization is to survive for any length of time. Just because the organization is not for profit does not mean it has any less need for success in each of these areas. Administration deals with overseeing the activities, ensuring the coordination and making certain there are adequate funds available to do the desired work. It is in the editorial area that publishing houses decide what to produce.

Acquisition and managing editors discuss and review ideas for books or articles. Large book publishers develop *trade lists* (a combination of prior publications, manuscripts in production and titles under contract) to achieve a profit while avoiding unnecessary competition with other publishers. Book selectors ought to learn something about the senior editors in the major publishing houses with which they deal. As with reviewing, the view of what is good or bad material is personal, so knowing the editors will help in planning selection activities. The editors' opinions about what to accept for publication determine what will be available.

Librarians and readers often complain that commercial publishers are exclusively, or at least overly, concerned with profit and have little concern for quality. What these people forget is that publishing houses are businesses and must show a profit if they are to continue to operate.

In 1998, *The New York Times* published an article about rising book production, loss of editors and the increase in errors in books. This article noted there was a 16 percent drop in the publishing workforce in New York City between 1990 and 1998 and that the decrease was primarily in the editorial category. It also speculated about the role mergers played in the situation. One editor was quoted as saying, "It's all become a big, fat, screaming, mean, vicious, greedy, rude and crude feast .... So little of your time is spent doing creative work that I'm seriously considering leaving". Editors are critical to the publishing process, so one hopes that the New York City situation is not representative of the field as a whole.

In fact, marketing departments are responsible for promoting and selling the product. They provide input about the sales potential of the title. Further, this unit often decides how many review copies to distribute and to what review sources. Where, when, or whether to place an aid are the responsibility of the marketing department. All of these decisions influence the cost of the items produced. Many small publishers use direct mail (catalogs and brochures) to market their books. Publishers' sales representatives visit stores, wholesalers, schools and libraries. When salespeople visit the library or information center, they keep the visits short and to the point.

Each visit represents a cost to the publisher and the company recovers the cost in some manner, most often in the price of the material. One activity for which most marketing units are responsible is exhibits. For library personnel, convention exhibits are one of the best places to meet publishers' representatives and have some input into the decision-making process. From the publishers' point of view, if the conferees go to the exhibits, conventions can be a cost-effective way of reaching a large number of potential customers in a brief time.

Librarians should also remember that the fees exhibitors pay help underwrite the cost of the convention. Fulfilment activities are those needed to process an order, including warehousing of the materials produced. In many ways, fulfilment is the least controllable cost factor for a publisher. Libraries and information centers sometimes add to the cost of their purchases by requiring special handling of their orders. Keeping special needs to a minimum can help keep prices in check. Speeding up payments to publishers and vendors will also help slow price increases, because the longer a publisher has to carry an outstanding account the more interest has to be paid.

Ultimately, most increases in the cost of doing business result in a higher price for the buyer, so whatever libraries can do to help publishers control their fulfilment costs will also help collection development budgets. For various reasons, despite strong marketing efforts, some publications do not sell as well as expected. When this happens, sooner or later the publisher has to dispose of the material; many times, these become remainders items.

A decision by the Internal Revenue Service has influenced press runs and the speed with which publishers remainder slow-moving warehouse stock (the *Thor Power Tool* decision. Remaindered items sell for a small fraction of their actual production cost. Prior to the *Thor* decision, businesses would write down the value of their inventories, or warehouse stock, to a nominal level at the end of the tax year. The resulting loss in the value of the inventory (which was, by and large, on paper only) then became a tax deduction for the company, increasing its profit. Since *Thor,* publishers can take such a deduction only if the material is defective or offered for sale below actual production cost. Under the previous method, publishers could find it profitable to keep slow-selling titles in their warehouses for years. Thus far, efforts to get an exemption from the ruling for publishers have been unsuccessful.

At first, the ruling increased the number of remaindered books, but now most publishers have cut back on the size of their print runs in an attempt to match inventories to sales volume. More often than not, this means higher unit costs and retail prices. Despite all the problems for the field, total net sales income for book publishing has increased steadily, from $14.1 billion in 1989 to an estimated $22.1 billion in 1998.

One can find data on annual sales in a variety of sources: *PW, The Bowker Annual of Library & Book Trade Almanac,* Standard and Poor's *Industry Surveys* and so forth. Anyone concerned with collection development must make use of statistical data about publishing to develop intelligent budgets and work plans. Statistical data about the number of new titles available as paperbacks, reprints and so forth, can be useful in planning the workload for the next fiscal year. For example, perhaps the library will need to hire more staff or redirect efforts of existing staff if the volume of acquisitions increases.

Knowing the pricing patterns over a period of years and the expected acquisitions budget allows one to project the workload. The two most accessible sources of publishing statistics for the United States are *PW* and *The Bowker Annual.* Data in both sources and almost all other printed statistical data about publishing, come from the American Book Producers Association (ABPA). Remember that the statistics represent information drawn from ABPA members and not all publishers belong to that group. In fact, a great many small and regional publishers do not. Publishers use a variety of distribution outlets, selling directly to individuals, institutions, retailers and wholesalers. Distribution is a major problem for both publishers and libraries because of the number of channels and the implications for acquiring a specific publication.

Each channel has a different discount and one accesses them through different sources. A general way the complexity of the system. Production and distribution of information materials, whether print or nonprint, consist of several elements, all interacting with one another. Writers and creators of the material can and do distribute their output in several ways: directly to the community or public, to agents who in turn pass it on to producers, or directly to the producers. Producers seeking writers often approach agents with publication ideas. The figure illustrates the variety of channels publishers use to distribute their publications to the consumer. Most publishers use all these sales channels. Wholesalers, direct mail companies and retail store operators act as middlemen; a retailer may buy from the jobber or directly from the publisher. Each seller will have different discounts for different categories of buyers, ranging from no discount to more than 50 percent.

Not only are there a great many choices available to the buyer, but the sources also compete with one another. These factors combine to push up the cost of distributing a publication, which in turn increases its list price. With multiple outlets, different discounts and different credit conditions, the publishing industry has created a cumbersome, uneconomical distribution system. Selling practices vary by title and publisher; however, one can make a few generalizations. Advertising will help a good book, but it seldom, if ever, makes a success out of a poor book. Publishers use both publicity and advertising, which are two different marketing devices. An interview with the author or a review of the book on a national radio or television program are examples of publicity. Normally free, publicity will do a great deal for the sales of a book.

However, the book's topic, or at least its author, must be of national interest or the title will not attract attention. Changes in current events can change a slow-moving book into a bestseller overnight, something that no amount of advertising can accomplish. As a general practice, publishers advertise in several ways. First, they use trade advertising directed toward retail outlets and institutional buyers. Second, they make an effort to get items reviewed in major professional and general review media. (Reviews are technically promotion rather than advertising, because one does not pay to have a title reviewed. However, a lead review can be worth more than a full-page advertisement). Third, they place announcements and ads. in professional journals, where the emphasis is on reaching individual buyers, both personal and institutional.

Fourth, they employ cooperative advertise-ments (co-op ads.) in the book review sections of many newspapers. A co-op ad. is one in which the publisher and a retail store share the cost of the advertisement. The publisher determines which titles are eligible for cooperative advertising. Finally, for books with a defined audience for which there is a good mailing list, the publisher often uses a direct mail campaign, again with individuals and institutional buyers as the targets.

Producers of Audiovisual Materials

Media producers are a diverse group working with a variety of formats (audio recordings, film, filmstrips, video, models and so on), making it difficult to generalize about their operations. The following discussion is an attempt to cover all of those audiovisual formats, but it would require a full-length book to describe all the individual variations and exceptions. Media producers enjoy substantial annual sales to schools and libraries. Indeed, this market is almost the sole sales outlet for the majority of media producers. Two major exceptions are audio and video recordings. The audio and video recording industries are the major sources of "other media" for most libraries. Recorded music, as part of a growing audio collection that includes talking books, is a common feature of libraries, reflecting the fact that a large segment of the general population buys or listens to music.

In terms of sales, however, libraries and other institutions represent only a fraction of the music industry's income. When one considers average circulations per title, video recordings are often the top circulation format, especially in public libraries. Video collections in libraries contain both educational and theatrical film recordings.

The sales of motion picture videocassettes to the general public are far larger than those to libraries, but libraries (including school media centers) are the largest market for educational video. One important fact to remember about most media, with the exception of books and filmstrips, is that they require the user to follow the material at a fixed pace—the pace of the machine involved.

Certainly, the equipment allows for rewinding and reviewing a section of special importance and video players can freeze a frame, but the formats make it difficult to skip around as one can do with a book. Selectors must keep this fact in mind when considering these formats for the collection. Will our typical user be able to benefit from the material, given the pace of presentation? Is a question for selectors to ponder. Interactive video and hypermedia allow for easy random access and these technologies are most likely to replace many of the traditional media formats libraries have made available. What newer format and technology will replace interactive systems is impossible to guess. Virtual reality is, to many people who follow developments in the field, an enhancement of interactive systems and not really a new "system". Most media producers design products for the average ability or level of knowledge of the target audience. In the case of educational media, the producer assumes that the item is for group presentations, with a teacher adding comments and creating a context for the material. Though individuals working alone can benefit from the material, many will gain less from use of the item without some interaction with an instructor.

More and more teachers in schools and higher education are assigning media use outside the classroom in the same way they have traditionally employed print material to supplement the instructional program. This translates into libraries and media centers receiving requests for bigger and more diverse media collections. The first major difference between book publishers and media producers is that media producers market a product designed primarily for group use and book publishers market a product designed primarily for individual use.

This difference has an influence on how media producers market and distribute their products. Media producers place heavy emphasis on direct institutional sales. Also, there is less use of wholesalers. Though some book jobbers do handle audio and video recordings, a large percentage of media acquisitions are made directly from the producer. One characteristic of media production that is frequently overlooked is authorship. Most books are the result of the intellectual effort of one or two persons. Textbook publishers frequently commission books. (Perhaps in the age of mergers, this approach will become more common for trade publications as well). For media, the process is the opposite. Normally, the producer generates the ideas and seeks the necessary persons to carry out the project if the company's staff cannot handle the project.

It is true that book publishers have the final say in what they will publish. The difference is that the book publisher receives hundreds of manuscripts and ideas for books to consider each year and thus has exposure to ideas and projects that otherwise might not receive consideration. In addition, even if one publisher rejects a manuscript, there is always the chance that another may pick it up. Book publishing has a tradition of being a free marketplace for ideas, whereas this concept is almost nonexistent in the media field. Although this may seem to be a subtle difference, it does have an effect on the type of material produced and, in turn, on the library's collection. Despite the producers' control, people often think of the media field as one of independence and freedom. One reason for this view is, at least in the past, the relatively low cost of entering it. One hears stories about the individual who started off with a few thousand dollars and some equipment and is now a major producer. One does not hear about the thousands of others who tried and failed. Mediocre equipment and a low advertising budget usually mean a mediocre product and few, if any, sales. The opportunity is there, but the chances of success are only slightly better than for any other business venture. Almost anyone may become a media producer; for example, to become a producer of 35mm slides (educational, art, travel and so forth), one needs only a 35mm camera, a stock of master images to use to produce slides on demand and some money for advertising.

Success is not likely, but this is all that one needs to become a media producer and be listed in a directory of media sources. In general, the start-up capital (money required to begin operations) is much lower than would be necessary for a book publisher. Good-quality professional media production equipment is exceedingly expensive; however, many of the so-called producers do not invest in quality equipment. They depend on commercial laboratories and hope for the best. Because of a lack of materials and the pressure to have media in schools and libraries, it has been and still is possible to sell copies of extremely poor-quality materials, because they are all that is available. All too often a selector must purchase an item on the basis of curriculum needs rather than on the basis of quality. Another characteristic of media producers is that their products have a fairly high cost per unit of information conveyed. Many media items are single-concept materials. (Single-concept films are a special class of educational films that deal with a very narrow concept, such as cell division and are usually very short, 3 to 4 minutes long). Books, in contrast, have a low cost per unit of information. For example, no single film, videotape, audiotape, or set of 35mm slides can convey the same amount of information about Native Americans as one 300-page book.

This feature of the media has great importance for selection, because not every medium is ideal for every purpose. Librarians must know the advantages of each medium and select and acquire items on this basis.

Though book publishers use a multitude of outlets to sell their products, media producers use few outlets. With the exception of audio and video stores and a few map shops, there are no retail outlets for "other media". There are no media-of-the-month clubs (except for music recordings and videos), few mail-order houses and no remainder houses (except for recordings and some videos). Even wholesalers dealing with all media are few and far between.

The main source and in some cases the only source, is the producer. Because the producers are the basic source, collection development personnel must spend an inordinate amount of time and energy maintaining lists of producers' addresses. Without such records, schools and libraries would almost have to halt their acquisition of "other media". Because many producers are small and move frequently, updating of addresses is a constant problem for the library. It means that directories more than 12 months old are likely to be out of date.

The one advantage to this situation is that the market for media is clearly identifiable: schools and libraries. Like the specialty publisher, the media producer is better able to focus advertising and sales activities on a small area with a high probability of success. Trade book publishers use a broad spectrum of advertising sources: newspapers, periodicals, flyers, radio and television. In general, the trade publisher must take a shotgun approach, but specialty publishers and media producers should have a much better idea of their market. Both books and other media are easy to copy. The difference is in the cost of the item. Most institutions capable of using media also have the capability to duplicate that material. That capability is a concern for producers because it was and still is, common to request to preview the material before placing a firm order. Previewing can be an opportunity for copying.

Awareness of this potential danger may be one factor

accounting for the general absence of media wholesalers. The media for which this danger is greatest are tapes (video and audio) and 35mm slides. The majority of media producers are small business owners without a large capital reserve. For the small media producer, cash flow is a real problem. Anything that the library can do to help the small media firm control its costs will help to control the unit cost of products as well (for example, using cooperative previewing and keeping ordering and billing procedures simple). One other important characteristic of the media field is the speed with which its technology changes. This characteristic is a central problem for everyone concerned, both producers and consumers.

Improvements in equipment constantly make existing equipment almost obsolete; occasionally, a new format may, in fact, make equipment obsolete. Given the volatile nature of the field, many users, with good reason, are reluctant to invest heavily in equipment.

For the producer, the problem is greater; it means deciding rather quickly whether to go with the new or stay with the old. On the one hand, staying with the old too long may cut the producer out of the field because of licensing, franchising considerations, or simply not keeping up-to-date.

'Problems and Collection Development'

It is to be noted that collection development personnel need to understand some of the important issues and problems facing producers, because those factors inevitably have an impact on their collections. Rising costs create problems for everyone, but publishers and media producers have some special problems. Information producers expenses pressure from two sides. On the one hand, the rising costs of materials and labor put pressure on them to raise the prices of their products.

On the other hand, if they do raise prices, they must realize that this may cut into sales, thus cutting into their profits more than the cost increases themselves. The consumer must meet basic needs first and during periods of inflation, meeting basic needs cuts into funds available for luxury items.

For most individual buyers, books and media are among the first items to be cut Producers are likely to continue increasing their prices as the personal buyer market continues to shrink. Institutional buyers will continue to buy materials, but a static materials budget over two or three years, in combination with increasing costs of materials, means that the library buys few items each year.

Most libraries do not receive large budget increases ever during inflationary periods. The increases they do receive do no more than keep pace with inflation; thus, for all practical purposes, the budget is static. These two factors effectively limit the number of items purchased and producers must carefully weigh these concerns before raising prices.

This, in turn, forces them to be more and more selective about the items they produce. They will carry few, if any, materials that do not show a profit. If producers could simplify their distribution system, they could achieve significant savings. Why should the general consumer individual or institution) be able to purchase an item directly from the producer or from a wholesaler or retailer? The distribution system as it now operates is cumbersome and costly. For book publishers, it is a matter of having a typical marketing system (producer to wholesaler to retailer), but at the same time the system allows any individual customer access to any level of the system to make a purchase. Media producers, in contrast, use direct sales.

Both systems are costly for everyone. The book system requires complex handling procedures at each level because of different classes of customers. For the media system, shipping single-item orders to numerous locations increases the cost of placing and filling an order. The impact on collection development is that more money goes into paperwork and administrative procedures and less is available to collection development. Both producers and librarians must strive to solve this problem. Perhaps the most difficult question concerns the right to use knowledge resources, or rather, how one may use them. As noted earlier, copyright has become a central issue among librarians, educators and other users of knowledge resources on the one hand and the producers on the other. Yet, without copyright, there is little incentive for anyone to produce a work. The problem is how far society can go to provide and protect such incentives and still ensure adequate access to material at a fair price. Libraries want open, free access and use and producers want limited free access. This issue, of course, has an important role to play in determining how one develops a collection, with electronic information making the issue ever more complex.

REFERENCES

Britt, B. "What Thou Lovest Well Remaindered". *Small Press* 10 (Winter 1991): 52-55.

Carter, R. A. "Taking Aim at the Library Market". *Publishers Weekly* 237 (June 8, 1990): S6-S12.

Dave, R. *The Private Press.* 2d ed. New York: R. R. Bowker, 1983.

Finn, M. "Everything You Need to Know About Trademarks and Publishing". *Publishers Weekly* 239 (January 6, 1991): 41-44.

Graham, G. "Publishers, Librarians and the Eternal Triangle". *Library Acquisitions: Practice and Theory* 15, no. 3 (1991): 261-64.

Grannis, C. B. *What Happens in Publishing?* 2d ed. New York: Columbia University Press, 1967.

Greco, Albert N. *The Book Publishing Industry.* Boston: Allyn & Bacon, 1997.

Hoffert, B. "Getting Published". *Library Journal* 115 (February 15, 1990): 153-56.

Hunter, K. A. "Making the Commercial Transition from Paper to Electronic: Or Publishing in the 'Twilight Zone.'" *Collection Management* 15, nos. 112 (1992) 129-39.

Kopka, M. "Backlist: How to Use It". *Publishers Weekly* 240 (October 4, 1993): 24-25.

Loe, M. K. H. "Book Culture and Book Business: U.K. vs. the U.S". *Journal of Academic Librarianship* 16 (March 1990): 4-10.

Newlin, B. "Traveling the New Information Superhighway". *Small Press* 12 (Spring 1994): 26-29.

One Book Five Ways. Los Altos, Calif.: William Kaufmann, 1977.

Posel, N. R. "High Priced or Over-Priced They're Every Library's Problem". *Reference Librarian* 19 (1987): 257-67.

Rettig, J. "Do Publishers Have Ears?" *Wilson Library Bulletin* 62 (January 1988) 15-22.

Salace, J. "Video Distribution: The Maze Made Manageable". *Library Journal* 115 (July 1990): 42-44.

Sexton, M. "Replacing the Myths About Marketing to Libraries". *Publishers Weekly* 236 (March 10, 1989): 56-57.

Taylor, S. A. "Joys of Electronic Togetherness". *Publishers Weekly* 240 (March 29, 1993): 24-28.

Weisberg, J. "Rough Trade: The Sad Decline of American Publishing". *New Republic* 204 (June 17, 1991): 16-21.

9

Flow Charting: As a Tool

> "One of the sadest things about human nature is, that a man may guide others in the path of life, without walking in it himself; that he may be a pilot, and yet a castaway."

Flow charting is an important tool at the hands of systems analyst in library and information science. Here it is apt to have a through understanding of the topic.

Why Flow Charting?

Flow charting is the symbolism of the systems analyst. By laying out facts in a common sense way it enables the analyst to view graphically partial or complete systems and to interpret analytically what may have been recorded only as a narrative procedure. Through the use of standardized flow-chart symbols a middle ground is created between the librarian and the systems analyst and efficient and effective communication may occur as a result of a properly constructed flow chart. Flow-chart symbols can be used to represent in a logical progression the elements (functions, decisions, and actions), the requirements, the inputs/outputs of the system, and the equipment used in the system.

Therefore the flow chart illustrates the sequential flow

of work and information through a system. The advantage of using flow charts stems from a system's being a process that is constantly changing; therefore in actual operation it is often difficult to understand without diagrams the relationships that exist within a system.

The flow chart may be compared to a series of snapshots stopping the action within a system allowing the analyst, systematically, and realistically, to evaluate the current operations and design new procedures if necessary. This is true because functions, decisions, and actions are clearly identified.

Symbols Used

The IBM X20-8020 flow-charting template symbols have been employed in the examples. These symbols may be readily used in either a machine or manual system. The construction of the flow chart may be accomplished by one of two methods: *(i)* progression from the top to the bottom of the chart-vertical-flow method; or *(ii)* moving from the left to the right in the chart—horizontal-flow method. Either approach has its merits and should not adversely affect the ability to interpret or construct the flow chart. However, once a method is adopted it should be consistently adhered to. These common symbols used to show the sequential flow of work are connected by directional flow lines with or without arrows.

Arrows only need be used when it is neces-sary to represent an exit or entry line from one symbol to another that is not in the same direction as the flow method being followed.

Special Purpose Symbols

The following symbols may be used when more detail

is desired or when the more specific symbols are readily applicable. They may also may be used in the flow charting of automated or computer systems.

Guidelines for Flow Charting

In practice, following general rules should be adhered to when preparing a flow chart:

1. Conventional symbols should be used to facilitate mutual understanding of the logical flow of work.
2. The system, or its components, or both, should have a clearly indicated starting and halting point in the chart.
3. The graphic flow of work should always be in one direction, normally top to bottom or left to right.
4. The descriptive statement within any symbol should be succinct and mutually understandable. The terminology used should be applicable to the system being studied.
5. No directional flow lines should be unconnected at any point. Every directional line should lead to another step in the chart.
6. Wherever ambiguity may be evident, annotation or side notes should be used to provide a thorough understanding of the various parts of the flow chart.
7. The flow of the work should be clearly indicative of what actually happens in the course of an operation. The realistic sequence of functions in the surveyed system should be followed throughout.
8. Each decision "diamond" should have two possibilities—a "yes' (positive) and a "no" (negative) path.
9. The analysis represented by the flow-chart should be consistent within itself. That is to say a flow

chart illustrating the process of a document through a system should not be expanded into representation of a clerk's functions having no bearing on the operation being charted.

10. Because the flow-charting of a complex system is an involved procedure, it is recommended that other staff members associated with the problem participate in the analysis phase of the flow charting operation.

Chart Construction

The "make-ready" phase of a flow chart is of vital importance in creating a picture that is representative of the system. Awareness of the component parts of the system to be flow charted is obviously required. With the aid of summary analyses and an understanding of procedures flow charting is facilitated and the analyst should become aware of the distinctiveness of each process and the individual decisions and flow paths that exist under the present procedure. In constructing the chart it is recommended that "pieces" of the system to be charted be written on individual slips of paper so that the initial arrangement of the flow-chart layout can be as flexible as possible. Once the arrangement is seen as satisfactory, the system can be transposed to sheet form.

For expediting the often necessary photocopying of the finished flow chart a standard paper size such as 8½ × 11 should be used.

Capabilities and Results

A flow chart pictographically representing a library system is uniquely capable of : (*a*) assisting in the organization of the system's structure; (*b*) helping to visualize the system's component parts; (*c*) Resulting in improved techniques, especially since the finished flow chart can be utilized as an effective training device with significant advantages over written job descriptions alone; and (*d*) helping in communication about and understanding of the system. At first in combination with the summary analyses and understanding of procedures the flow-charts should show the existing system with all of its characteristic faults and strengths.

One certain proof of the validity of an existing system is whether it can be flow charted effectively at all. If not, the system must be illogical. By surveying the input to any entry point in the system the analyst as he proceeds step by step through the flow chart can see the uses that will be made of the input, what decisions must be made, how the input affects the decisions, and what action comes from each decision. Thus he can judge whether the decisions are correctly made in relation to the requirements placed against the system.

He also can evaluate what effect various demands would have on decisions and their related actions in order to develop the set of criteria or managerial procedures that best satisfies the system's requirements. With the standard rate for each function available, the analyst is in a position to analyze those operations appearing to be overburdened or near breakdown at certain steps depicted in the flow chart.

He can then evaluate and suggest alternate paths to be taken, if any, to maximize the system's effectiveness. An evaluation representative of a "before" and "after" library binding procedure. The basic question to ask in evaluating each of the flow chart's parts would be the possibility of simplifying, eliminating, combining, or rearranging any of the elements of the work flow shown. The results of the overall evaluation are to be used as the basis of a flow chart serving to suggest new and improved methods of accomplishing the operation under study. These suggested methods will involve major or minor changes according to the past operational success or failure of the present system.

The new or improved methods will also depend on the resources available. If any automation is planned, a concept of vital importance in suggesting revision of a system is the establishment of manual procedures and operations that will be machine compatible.

The above discussion makes it clear that flow charts can help library professionals in big way. This may systematise their functions and workability.

10

Automated Circulation System

In common parlance the phrase "total system," as used here, concerns itself with more than the immediate library system or the overall parent administrative system. Rather it is meant to designate the symbiotic relationships within the library and the general relationships of the library with society; that is, it is meant to deal with the interrelationships or interdependence among systems that affect one another and in many instances justify and facilitate the existence and performance of systems. Interdependence is the key word describing the inner workings of systems within a total system.

General society, all inclusive, is the source not only for the people who are to manage the library but also for the library users and the supply of outside supporting services and materials to the library. When viewed in closer perspective the interdependent systems of the library. Stylized, relationships between the systems within the total library are shown encompassed by the administration and planning system. Circulation is depicted as logically interrelated with the reference system and the cataloging system. From the latter newly processed library materials are received and controlled by the circulation system in order to provide the library's users with ready access.

The location symbols assigned and indexes prepared and maintained by cataloging are used by the circulation system and by the library users to locate and relocate desired items. One of the relationships between acquisitions and cataloging in which the one furnishes the material for the other to process so as to make it readily accessible to the library user and to other systems, further serves as an illustration of the total systems concept.

Reciprocally the records that cataloging maintains allow acquisitions to search each purchase request effectively before ordering to avoid unwanted duplication of material work.

When the circulation system is accepted as a system that is directly interdependent with other systems within the library as well as with outside systems (that is, the user), a more lucid understanding of the place of the circulation system within the total library system may be realized. It should also become increasingly clear that the design of a new system with its stated demands and requirements and its inputs/outputs will have direct bearing in varying degree on all the other systems within the total system.

Therefore it becomes very important in designing a new system to be fully aware of what immediate and long-term effects a new printed form, method or procedure will have on existing cosystems.

In considering the design of a computer-based loan system it should at least be able to emulate the worthwhile elements of the existing systems.

These elements, probably common to all circulation systems, include the ability to:

1. Indicate what book is out and who has it.
2. Indicate the date the book was taken out and the date it is to be returned.
3. Allow for a daily count of circulation activity by type of material and possibly by the status of the user.
4. Search for missing books, and if found or not, notify the requestor of the book's availability.
5. Allow for reserving charged-out library material.
6. Charge out and discharge library material.
7. Maintain records of overdue books and issue notices as required.
8. Allow for a daily updating of the master file of outstanding circulation by interfiling the daily transactions.
9. Provide on users' notices the call number, title, and due date of the requested material.
10. Enable the library to know the user's identify prior to borrowing any material.
11. Facilitate recall of charged-out material prior to its due date.

Accepting the necessity for maintaining the objectives of the existing circulation system, the computer-based system could be designed by the analyst to gain a variety of improvements in the maintenance and accessibility of circulation records and more meaningful statistical records. In addition to improving on present objectives the computer-based circulation system should be designed to be flexible enough to:

1. Answer a user's enquiry as to the status of a book (out, in, missing) by current printouts arranged

variously by author or title, call number, and borrower, including in each listing the date the material was charged out and is to be returned.

2. Ascertain the user's identity and be able to correlate by statistical analysis, his subject background with the type of material he charges out.
3. Provide work-unit statistics to indicate hourly and daily workloads.
4. Maintain a historical file of loan transaction records for use in periodic statistical studies.
5. Be as mechanical as possible in its charge and discharge operations so as not to be dependent to any appreciate extent on manual keying or writing functions and thus make charge and discharge operations as rapid and free of error as possible.
6. Allow for *portable* terminal data collection devices for use in inventorying the book collection and perhaps to allow for user self-charging of material.
7. Take into account short circulation periods, anywhere from a few minutes to several hours, allowing for class reserve books to be controlled by the computer-based circulation system. (This may be best performed in an on-line system).
8. Provide for continuing analysis of the book collection by frequency of use by subject and subject background of user so as to evaluate collection growth and adequacy.
9. Indicate the retrospective and current number of uses of any book within the library's collection to facilitate the ordering of additional copies of materials or the weeding out of inactive material.

10. Permit expeditious inventorying of the collection with machine readable records.
11. Machine produce on request and as needed recall and overdue notices.
12. Maintain statistical records of user requests for missing books.
13. Be able to generate on request lists of books charged to individual users.
14. Allow for conversion to an online circulation system.
15. Analyze the use made of class reserve reading material.

Remarkably, only should the systems analyst be aware of what objectives the circulation system should fulfill, he should also be able to evaluate the commercially available mechanical data collection (input) devices best suited to realize the total systems concepts in the computer-based circulation system. Along with the decision made regarding the type of input devices to be used to capture the transaction record, a master punched book card (the input) for each circulating item, probably an 80-column punched card, should be produced with enough information to identify the book. If the bibliographic data is already computer based, it is only a matter of stripping the necessary information from the existing computer record and producing the punched bok card, interpreting the Hollerith code to make the card man-readable, and inserting it into the book. An example of planning for the future is provided in the case of the library system that has used no book cards, even under the manual system, but still provided a book card pocket in the back of each book in the planned event that punched cards would be used as master book cards in a computer-based circulation system. If the cataloging system is at present converting its records to machine-readable form, the master book card could be an economical by-product of the conversation process. As the shelf list is converted selected information would be punched into the punched card to create a master book card could for the circulation system.

If no machine-readable bibliographic records exist, the conversion of records to machine-readable form to produce the master book cards is a costly and critical operation prior to the implementation of the computer-based circulation system.

Master Book Card

Provided that a machine-readable record can be produced, the analyst should define the data to be carried on each master book card. He has less than 80 columns with which to uniquely identify the book because some of the card space is allocated for the identification number of the user, which will appear on the transaction card combined with the data from the master book card.

Therefore the information contained in the master book card and that added to the transaction card, although minimal, should allow for:

1. Positive identification of the specific book by the master book card. The order or accession number or the full call number, or both, including volume, part, copy, and so forth, would appear to be necessary.
2. Enough bibliographic information to enable the user and the library staff to identify the book by author or title, or both, in a printout list of loan transactions. It may not be necessary for this

information to be punched into the master book card because a machine-readable shelf list in computer storage can be used either in real-time (immediate access) or in an off-line situation for complete identification of the book if the call number or the order number is used as the key to the entire bibliographic record.

3. The due date; the computer programme can take this into account and provide the due date on the printout.

User Identification Card

The data to be carried by the machine-readable user identification card should be specified by the analyst. If properly designed, this card serves as an excellent example of application of the total systems design concept. For the purposes of the library the identification card would be Hollerith coded with some identifying number that would serve as the key to each user's name and address and other pertinent information in a separate machine-readable file. This key number, which would be punched into the user's card, should have certain characteristics:

1. It should be short enough for the identification card and for the remaining space on the master book card when combined in a transaction card.
2. It also should take into account the accessibility of already existing machine-readable borrower files or other machine-readable files carrying this type of information that could be used to provide addresses and other data for collection development studies. If no machine-readable files exist, it is a matter of converting manual borrower or user files.

An identification card to be carried by each user should be provided or an existing card modified to meet the demands of the new system. This card requires key punching and if this is not amenable to an already existing card, a new one will be needed.

If a new identification card is required, it should be designed to carry: (i) positive identification of the user by a photograph, name, the Hollerith coded identification number, and possibly the person's signature and (ii) any additional information that is compatible with other uses of the card outside of the library. In support of the total systems concept the identification card should be designed to be useful, if possible, in other systems.

By embossing the name and birthdate of the carrier on the card it can be used as a "charge plate"; and by providing a photograph and signature it can serve as a very compact general-use identification card. In a university situation such a card would find application in library, bookstore, registration, and student activities transactions. The most important characteristic of identification number to be punched into the card is the adaptability it will or should have in existing machine-readable identification files in various systems. Therefore special consideration should be given to the machine-readable number to be used: is it to be a locally unique number or a nationally unique one like the Social Security number?

In support of the nationally unique number the implications of the increasing interest and activity in shared library resources indicate the need for universal identification. For example, in a network of libraries if a number of the cooperating libraries implement computer-based circulation systems and users from any one of these borrow books from various libraries in the system, the identification number should be machine-compatible throughout the system. This obviously necessitates a machine-readable central address file accessible to the cooperating libraries.

The format and content of the master book card and user identification are important to the contributions of the circulation system to the total library systems goals. This is in terms of the circulation system's ability to contribute effectively to the administration of the library and to collection development for best service to users. If a library is to capitalize on the statistical information available from daily circulation transaction records, some planned means of making use of this data should be provided.

The materials circulated are obviously an indication of user subject and intellectual interests and development. A variety of statistical records can be supplied by a functionally designed computer-based circulation system. Continuing statistical analysis can serve to signal and predict fluctuations in demands being placed on the library. Therefore data collection as a by-product of the circulation control system should be designed to be sensitive to the subtle changes in user requirements and expectations. The result of such an approach will verify the aptness of the techniques already in use to attain the library's service goals or it may show the conventional techniques to be inadequate. In order to analyze properly information gathered the data collection function needs to be designed to: (i) incorporate flexibility and compatibility in the gathered data to generate needed reports; (ii) balance economic limitations against statistical reports clearly required in terms of the broadness of their application; and (iii) consider the needs and demands of the user, the types of users, and the ecology of the library.

Data Collection Device

The mechanical input device in a computer-based loan system should be able to generate the necessary data for computer input. Apart from expeditiously accepting and processing the inserted master book card and the user's card, the machine should be able to withstand extensive use in repeated charging and discharging functions. It would seem that the more simple the machine's construction and the more independent it is of auxiliary equipment, the less chance there is of it failing. It should have the feature of being able to go on line.

Regarding the routine operations in which the machine will be involved, the discharging of books may be a problem area under certain conditions. In a one-card system the master card is used to produce the charge and discharge record for the input to the computer and in doing so requires that the book always stay with the master card. As a solution to this problem a two-card system produced by the input device is suggested. Two cards are produced from the master book card : (i) a charge-out card that contains the same data as the transaction card and is placed in the book pocket along with the master card; and (ii) a transaction record card that serves as computer input. By this method the charge card can be removed from the returned book and the book sent immediately to the selves. The charge-out card serves to clear the computer record by matching with the transaction record as it appears in the computer.

By defining the necessary data to be incorporated in each master book card and user card the analyst should be able to extract a number of valuable statistical use studies and measures from the loan record. For example, because there are no precise means of ascertaining stack or in house use of books, those charged out should have significance in measuring the use of the collection and in collection development. Because the computer can readily provide records of actual use and non-use of books, this has direct bearing on collection development by the reference system. If a subject represented by a group of books is no longer referred to, the purchase of new materials in that subject field may be questioned. Effective collection development through awareness of use should also provide data for subject profiles of specialized users, augmented and confirmed by personal interviews. If circulation records reveal that a title is used extensively, additional copies may be automatically purchased.

Within the cumulative circulation statistical record, book use can be measured and classified by call number and perhaps, preferably, by means of the subject "tracings" in the computerized shelf list correlated with the subject background of users. From observation of circulation trends suggested reading lists of currently appearing titles could be produced as an awareness service in the subject areas of readers' interests. Through the use of statistics it would be possible to predict inductively by any subject's use or non-use the significant growth or decline of interest by library users. This could be a direct aid in the library's book-selection subsystem.

In most, if not all libraries, the administration is in competition for increased budgets with other units and offices of the governing administration. The library administration should be able to demonstrate through quantitative and qualitative use records of the library's collection the need for an increased book budget. These use studies may also indicate need for a decrease in or shifting of acquisitions funds that may have been wanted in maintaining unused subject collections.

An additional operation that would be dependent on a computer-based circulation record and shelf list would be that of inventorying the collection entirely or on a sampling basis. Records of user queries foe missing books in a given area might indicate the need for an inventory of that area.

Remarkably, implied previously circulation transaction records are one of the best sources of information about collection-use patterns. Other means of ascertaining use, including on-site observation and the counting of unshelved books on tables, may be too limited and may not cover the overall aspects that an extensive collection of computerized circulation records could provide. The percentage of books ten years old or older found on study tables in a two-week period and used as the basis to extrapolate a general statement on the entire collection's use does not necessarily provide sufficient guidance for weeding of a collection. Under the total-system concept and the management by exception principle all facets of collection use are considered or may be considered.

This reveals not only the extent of use of older books but also an itemized listing of these books, their subjects background of their users. By exploiting the full capability of loan statistics to measure and project library use, service to groups of library users may be improved. The current loan transaction indicates what is happening and there by may allow the library's administration to respond to the demands of the library's users as deduced from the loan statistics. If a definitive pattern can be obtained about how effective the library is in meeting user requirements, far more precise parameters of library service may be established.

A further illustration of the total systems concept is

the loan transaction record accumulated over a period of time; this could be very meaningful in arriving at staff subject specialist requirements. The nature of the user, derived from subject profile analyses by questionnaire and personal interviews as well as from actual use reports, would provide a guide to the subject background and experience needed for meeting the needs of the library's community. Although this would be only a partial measurement, it would still contribute to a broader understanding of job requirements.

The analyst in designing a system utilizing the total systems concept not only should be aware of what effect the design will have on other systems but also should be cognizant of and prepared for new technological developments. A computer-based circulation system should be designed to take into account on-line operating procedures. By an on-line operation is meant direct input to the computer, usually with immediate response from the computer. Printouts may still be used as guides to the out-standing circulation. An on-line procedure makes unneces-sary the preparation of the computer input, the transaction card of the master book card's data combined with user's identification.

11

Censorship and Intellectual Freedom

Here in this chapter we will make an attempt to fully explore all the aspects of intellectual freedom and free speech. Although they are interesting and important concepts for anyone involved in collection development, they are so complex that each has been the subject of numerous books and articles. All librarians must have an understanding of these areas, but it is essential that all selection personnel fully comprehend the issues relating to censorship.

Many library associations have membership-approved statements and public positions on the questions of free speech and intellectual freedom. The ALA's "Freedom to Read" Statement is a classic example. Most of the statements contain fine-sounding phrases. The statements *look* useful when one is discussing the theory or philosophy of intellectual freedom in the classroom or in a meeting. However, on a daily basis, these statements provide little assistance in collection development and provide only limited assistance in fighting off a censor. Usually, intellectual freedom and free speech controversies revolve around interpretations of points of law and possible violations of existing law. Therefore, the fight normally involves attorneys and judges rather than librarians and the community. We hear about the cases that reach the courts, but seldom about daily local problems.

Cases often start as local problems between the library and an individual or group from the community and are usually settled quickly. Most often, the problem arises when some-one objects to an item already in the collection. Depending on the nature of the material, the level of emotional involvement, and the prior administrative actions (that is, policies), the library may be able to quickly resolve the issue, or the problem may escalate until it reaches the courtroom.

1. Staff with an excellent background in interpersonal relations
2. A lack of action for handling complaints
3. A lack of strong feelings on the part of the person making the complaint
4. A lack of concerted pressure from special-interest groups
5. Available backup material from library associations

If the individual making a complaint believes very strongly in the matter, it is likely that the library's attorney will become involved. From that point on, depending on the emotional involvement and financial resources, the issue may go from the lowest to the highest court in the country before the problem is resolved. The local issue usually is censorship. Charles Busha provided a satisfactory definition of *censorship* as it concerns the library: "The rejection by a library authority of a book (or other material) which the librarian, the library board or some person (or persons) bringing pressure on them holds to be obscene, dangerously radical, subversive, or too critical of the existing mores" (Beginning selection officers should read the Busha article.) Censorship has been a problem for librarians as long as there have been libraries. Generally speaking, librarians attempt to resist censorship. (No one knows how many times a librarians or information officer responds to a complaint by removing the offensive item because he or she agrees that it is offensive.) Evidence suggests a difference between librarians' attitudes toward the concept of censorship and their behaviour in handling censorship problems. An article by one of the gadflies of librarianship, Sandy Berman, outlined some of his ideas about "self censorship."

Librarians' success in fending off censors' efforts varies-there are both notable successes and spectacular failures. The sad truth is that there are no rules or guidelines that ensure success. It is possible to forestall many complaints and quickly resolve those that do occur; however, there is always a chance that the procedures and processes will and a legal battle will ensue.

Why Censorship?

Motives may be psychological, political, or social in nature. Psychological motives stem from the desire to restrain others from expressing ideas or creating works that the censor finds offensive. Political motivation underlies the actions of governments that attempt to maintain control over the communication systems that may threaten the government or its policies. Social motivations spring from a desire to preserve a wholesome social setting or to reduce crime, both of which the censor may consider related to the presence of objectionable material in the library.

Frequently, the censor (government, groups, or an individual) claims to be acting for "protective" reasons. Censorship is a paternalistic act in that it limits the experiences of both adults and children and limits environments to influences acceptable to the censor. Freedom and censorship exist in opposition. At one extreme, some persons believe there should be no controls; if they could, they would eradicate all laws, rules, and regulations. At the other extreme are those who think everyone needs protection and outside control. Between these extremes lies the necessary balance between freedom and restraint.

Freedom must be restrained so that social institutions can intelligently protect citizens' rights and ensure individual's free choice. Librarians work on a daily basis to achieve an appropriate balance in their collections and services. The ALA adopted a Library Bill of Rights in 1948. ALA's Office for intellectual Freedom (OIF) vigorously promotes and publicizes the concepts contained in that statement. Because the Library Bill of Rights is not law, the statement provides no legal protection for libraries or librarians. What legal protection exists is primarily in the freedom-of-speech provisions of the First Amendment to the United States Constitution. The First Amendment grants every U.S. citizen the right of freely express opinions in speech, writing, or with graphics; to distribute them; and to seek information from public sources without unnecessary restraint.

The Library Bill of Rights outlines the basic freedom-of-access concepts that the ALA hopes will guide library public service. It states that persons should be able to read what they wish without intervention from groups or individuals—including librarians. Since its adoption in 1948, the provisions of the Library Bill of Rights have assisted librarians in committing their libraries to a philosophy of service based on the premise that users of libraries should have access to information on all sides of all issues. The text of the document, as amended February 2, 1961; June

27, 1967; and January 23, 1980; and reafirmed in 1996 by the ALA Council.

The American Library Association affirms that all libraries are forums for information and ideas, and that the following basic policies should guide their services.

I. Books and other library resources should be provided for the interest, information, and enlightenment of all people of the community the library serves. Materials should not be excluded because of the origin, background, or views of those contributing to their creation.

II. Libraries should provide materials and information presenting all points of view on current and historical issues. Materials should not be proscribed or removed because of partisan or doctrinal disapproval.

III. Libraries should challenge censorship in the fulfillment of their responsibility to provide information and enlightenment.

IV. Libraries should cooperate with all persons and groups concerned with resisting abridgment of free expression and free access to ideas.

V. A person's right to use a library should not be denied or abridged because of origin, age, background, or views.

VI. Libraries which make exhibit spaces and meeting rooms available to the public they serve should make such facilities available on an equitable basis, regardless of the beliefs or affiliations of individuals or groups requesting their use.

Adopted June 18, 1948
Amended February 2, 1961, and January 23, 1980,
inclusion of "age" reaffirmed January 23, 1996,
by the ALA Council.

The Library Bill of Rights is an important guide to professional conduct in terms of intellectual freedom. It is a standard by which one can gauge daily practices against desired professional behaviour in the realms of freedom of access to information, communications, and intellectual activity.

Despite the Library Bill of Rights, there is pressure to limit or exclude certain types of material from a library's collection. Occasionally, someone suggests labeling material with warnings or some kind of rating system rather than removing it. This practice usually takes the form of placing special marks or designations (stars, letters, and so forth) on certain classes of materials. The practice of labeling is prejudicial and creates bias.

Labeling is a defensive method that says, in effect, "This item may not meet with full community approval". Labelling is contrary to the principles of intellectual freedom. It is not the librarian's duty to warn readers against such things as obscene language; descriptions of explicit sexual acts; or unorthodox political, religious, moral, or economic theories.

Librarians are preservers and providers rather than censors. Librarians must always bear in mind that many intellectual advances, in all fields, involve controversy. A librarian's primary responsibility is to provide, not restrict, access to information. Thus, the ALA's position is against labeling materials, in the sense of warning people about the content of items. In 1951, ALA adopted an anti-labeling statement, which it last amended on June 26, 1990.

The ALA statements provide a philosophical base for resisting censorship. However, in the long run, success or failure depends on the individual librarian's personal beliefs and attitudes. ALA's Office of Intellectual Freedom has a variety of publications and position statements that can assist libraries in handling issues of intellectual freedom, censorship, access to materials, and so forth.

Types of Censorship

A librarian or information professional may encounter three forms of censorship: legal or governmental, individual or group, and self-censorship. The first two are easier to respond to than the third. For the first type, there are two choices: comply or fight. Usually, fighting to change a low or interpretation of a law is time-consuming and expensive. Because of the time and cost involved, a single librarian or library seldom attempts it.

Even at the community level involving a local ordinance, if there is to be a modification, there must be community-wide support. The library staff working alone has little chance of success. Literary censorship has existed for a long time. The United States has seen an interesting mix of individual and governmental censorship. Anthony Comstock was a person of strong beliefs and personality whose efforts to control the reading materials of Americans were so vigorous and successful that his name is now part of the lexicon of intellectual freedom and censorship discussion—Comstockery.

No doubt, Comstock was so vocal in his efforts that, in 1873, Congress passed a law that attempted to create a structure for national morality. For almost 75 years, this law went unchallenged, with the U.S. Postal Service designated as the government agency primarily responsible for enforcement at the national level. At the local level, several elements were at work. State and local governments passed similar regulations, and, thus, local police departments became involved in the control of vice. Law enforcement agencies had ample help from two citizen groups: the Society for the Suppression of Vice and the Watch and Ward Society.

The "Society for the Suppression of Vice" was the vehicle Comstock used to gain popular support and to show the depth of national support for his views. A primary activity of the society was checking on printed material available to local citizens, whatever the source (bookstores, newsstand, and libraries both public and private). Occasionally, when the society felt that local law enforcement official were not moving quickly enough, it took matters into its own hands.

> Labeling is the practice of describing or designating materials by affixing a prejudicial label and/or segregating them by a prejudicial system. The American Library Association opposes these means of predisposing people's attitudes toward library materials for the following reasons:
>
> 1. Labelling is an attempt to prejudice attitudes and as such, it is a censor's tool.
> 2. Some find it easy and even proper, according to their ethics, to establish criteria for judging publications as objection-able. However, injustice and ignorance rather than justice and enlightenment result from such practices, and the American Library Association opposes the establishment of such criteria.
> 3. Libraries do not advocate the ideas found in their collections. The presence of books and other resources in a library does not indicate endorsement of their contents by the library.
>
> A variety of private organisations promulgate rating systems and/or review materials as a means of advising either their members or the general public concerning

their opinions of the contents and suitability or appropriate age for use of certain books, films, recordings, or other materials. For the library to adopt or enforce any of these private systems, to attach such ratings to library materials, to include them in bibliographic records, library catalogs, or other findings aids, or otherwise to endorse them would violate the Library Bill of Rights.

While some attempts have been made to adopt these systems into law, the constitutionality of such measures is extremely questionable. If such legislation is passed which applies within a library's jurisdiction, the library should seek competent legal advice concerning its applicability to library operations.

Publishers, industry groups, and distributors sometimes add ratings to material or include them as part of their packaging. Librarians should not endorse such practices. However, removing or obliterating such ratings—if placed there by or with permission of the copyright holder—could constitute expurgation, which is also unacceptable.

The American Library Association opposes efforts which aim at closing any path to knowledge. This statement, however, does not exclude the adoption of organisational schemes designed as directional aids or to faclitate access to materials.

Adopted July 13, 1951. Amended June 25, 1971; July 1, 1981; June 26, 1990, by the ALA Council.

Book burnings did take place, and the society applied pressure to anyone involved in buying or selling printed material to stock only items it deemed moral. The phrase "banned in Boston" originated as a result of the society's activity. From 1873 until well into the twentieth century, the United States experienced a mix of all three types of censorship: official censorship because of the 1873 law;

group pressure from organized societies concerned with the moral standards of their communities; and self-censorship on the part of publishers, booksellers, and librarians. A public or even a private stance by librarians against such censorship was almost unheard of; in fact, professional groups sponsored workshops and seminars to help librarians identify improper books.

Most of the notable librarians of the past are on record (in ALA proceedings, speeches, or writings) in favour of this type of collection development. As E. Geller noted, Arthur Bostwick felt it was reasonable to purchase books like *Man and Superman* for the New York Library's reference collection (noncirculating), but not for branch libraries. Bostwick's inaugural speech as president of the ALA (1908) was about the librarians censor; as censor the librarian performed a positive act, if not an fact of "greatness," Bostwick said.

An interesting situation arose with foreign-language titles. Many authors were available in their own language, but not in English. Apparently, if one was could read French, German, Spanish, Russian, or any other language, one was reading a "moral" book-but that same work in an English translation was immoral. The censorial atmosphere caused a few American authors to live abroad, and some had a larger foreign readership than English-speaking readership. At the time, librarians were no more vocal in protesting this situation than anyone else in the country.

The period between 1873 and the mid-1950s exhibited all of the censorship problems one can encounter. From the 1930s to the mid-1950s, various federal court decisions, including several by the U.S. Supreme Court, slowly modified the 1873 law. The 1873 Comstock Act remains a part of the U.S. Code, but it is no modified as to be a completely different law. Most court cases dealing with censorship were between the government and publishers or booksellers. Librarians and their associations occasionally entered the suits as *amici curiae* (friends of the court) but seldom as defendants or plaintiffs. Major changes in the interpretation of the law began with the U.S. Supreme Court's 1957 *Roth* decision. This decision established a three-part test for obscenity. First, the dominant theme of the work as a whole had to appeal to a prurient interest in sex.

Second, the work had to be patently offensive because it affronted contemporary community standards in its representation of sex. Third, the work had to be utterly without redeeming social value. With that interpretation, more sexually explicit material became available in the open market. Not unexpectedly, some people objected to the new openness, and in 1973, the Supreme Court, in deciding the *Miller* case, modified the three-part test. The court suggested a new three-part test. First, would an average person applying contemporary community standards find that the work as a whole appealed to prurient interest in sex?

Second, does the work depict or describe in a patently offensive way sexual conduct specifically prohibited in a state's law? Third, does the work, as a whole, lack serious literary, artistic, political, or scientific mores by employing tests that emphasize local standards.

This test is in place today. Does the shift in emphasis matter? Yes, especially in terms of production and distribution of materials. One example of what the changed interpretation could do to distribution occurred in 1982. *Show Me: A Picture Book of Sex, for Children and Parents* (New York: St Martin's Press, 1975), a children's book by Will McBride, was taken out of distribution by its American publisher/distributor, St. Martin's Press. It stopped distribution because the U.S. Supreme Court upheld a New York state child pornography law. The book contained photographs of nude children. The New York law contained a strict provision barring the use of children in all sexually explicit films and photographs, obscene or not. St. Martin's had already successfully defended *Show Me* in Massahusetts, New Hampshire, and Oklahoma. However, the publisher decided that determining which of the 50 states it could legally ship the book to, as well as keeping track of individual orders, was much too difficult, so it stooped all distribution. Perhaps the most interesting aspect of this incident is that the book was written by a Swiss child psychologist (Helga Fleischhauer-Hardt) and the photographs were taken by an American photographer (Will Mcride). They prepared the book for a Lutheran church-sponsored children's book company in West Germany in 1974. The English-language edition appeared in 1975, and St. Martin's stated that it has sold almost 150,000 copies in hardback and paperback before it ceased distribution.

Some distributors and book clubs started using labeling systems in an attempt to protect themselves from lawsuits. For example, one book club used labels that state: "Warning: explicit violence" or "Warning: explicit sex and violence." A few people speculated that the purpose was to increase sales rather than avoid a lawsuit. Perhaps it served a dual purpose. For a time, one of the library distributors that serves many school media centers included warnings with "problem" books it shipped. For example, in children's books acquired for courses in children's literature, librarians at Loyola Marymount University have found slips bearing the warning, "This book is not up to our usual standards." Such labeling violates the ALA Statement on Labeling; however, it also reflects the growing concern on the part of vendors with social and with pressures to influence those values. Today, just as during the period 1873-1950, most of the problems libraries encounter are with individual and group attempts to censor material. Although no active "Society for the Suppression of Vice" exists today, librarians increasingly face organized pressure groups. What may at first seem to be a person's objection to one book can became a major confrontation between a library and an organized pressure group. Much depends on the energy and time that the would-be censor is willing to devote to the issue. Influential persons may be able to organize a group to generate even greater pressure than the average person could.

A librarian may encounter organized pressure groups based on local interests and views (often, views that are religious or politically oriented), but seldom does a librarian face a challenge from a local group with broad national support. If such a group were to exist, it would be extremely difficult to avoid at least an occasional debate (if not an all-out battle) over some materials in the collection. Policy statements about controversial materials, the ALA's Freedom to Read documents, and other support materials will help to slow the process, but they will not stop it.

Local groups are particularly hard to resist, because they can have a fairly broad base of community support and their existence indicates some active interest in certain problems. A few examples illustrate the problems that confronted many librarians in the United States during the 1990s. One example was found in a 1993 report about censorship in U.S. schools.

The report, released by People for the American Way, indicated that in 41 percent of the 395 reported attempts at censorship, censors succeeded in having the objectionable material removed or restricted in some manner.

The report indicated that the majority of the reported attempts were by groups identified as religious right or "pro-family."

It went on to report school personnel as acknowledging that they were being careful in what they added to the collections, a form of self-censorship. A 1983-1984 study indicated that school media centers resolved most challenges without removing the item or restricting access. In 1992, ALA's Office for Intellectual Freedom recorded 653 incidents; however, it believes that libraries report less than 15 percent of all attempts.

Much of the censorship pressure arises from a concern about children, and the concern is not limited to sex. Some parents do not believe they are capable of judging the materials that their children are exposed to in school or the library. As a result, several organizations review materials for worried parents. These reviewers are particularly active in the area of elementary school textbooks and required reading material, but they also assess what is in the general collections that support the curriculum.

Supporters of biblical creationism suggest that libraries are censoring Christian materials and especially creationism literature (or creation science.). Anyone thinking about going into school media center work needs to be fully aware of what is taking place and to beware the dangers and pitfalls. Court, which limited the power of school boards to limit access to materials, did not solve all the problems. Not all censors are concerned about children's welfare. Challenges to materials based on their racist or sexist content arise fairly often. One of the more unusual cases was "*The Incredible Case of the Stack O' Wheat Murders*" photograph incident in 1980. The case illustrates that censorship battles are not limited to public and school libraries. The Stack o' Wheat incident occurred in the special collections room at the University of California, Santa Cruz library. Ten 4-×-5-inch photographs, called "*The Incredible Case of the Stack o' Wheat Murders*," were taken by photographer Les Krims. The collection was a parody of theme murders intended for use in a marketing project. Each photograph showed a "gruesomely" murdered nude woman dripping blood alongside a stack of wheat pancakes.

The dripping blood was chocolate syrup; the chocolate represented the "epitome of the series humour," according to the text that accompanied the photographs. A young woman who viewed the photographs demanded their removal from the library's collection on the ground that they represented the sexploitation of woman. When the library took no action, she went to the special collections room, ripped up the photographs and accompanying material, and poured chocolate syrup over the debris. The case quickly escalated into a significant problem for the campus, encompassing many complex issues, such as freedom of expression, censorship, status of woman, vandalism, and social justice. Another, more recent case involving photographs, one that gained national attention, was the Robert Mapplethorpe controversy, This case went to trial and led to the resignation of a museum director, as well as an individual who had once won ALA's intellectual freedom awards.

If nothing else, these cases illustrate how deeply a censorship issue can divide a community. When local pressure groups exist, the librarian may ask, "How will they react if I buy this item?" Thinking along these lines allows one to deal with one's worries. The real danger in the situation is when the thought is unconscious. At that point, the pressure group has almost accomplished its purpose, that is, control over what goes into the collection. Further, the group has accomplished it through the librarian's self-censorship.

Self-censorship is our greatest problem as librarians and information professionals. We all believe that we would never censor ourselves, but it is difficult to prevent. A few librarians would agree with Walter Brahm; it is better to retreat and fight another day. He reasoned that censorship falls victim to the times; that public opinion can only dampen censorship; that over time, no one can lead society's mores in directions the population opposes. Certainly, libraries and librarians cannot accomplish this alone, and generally, libraries are not the main battleground of intellectual freedom.

Most librarians would take a public stance against Brahm's position, when stated in a theoretical sense and when it does not affect them directly. When it becomes a real issue and there is personal involvement, it becomes another matter.

Journals

In the late 1990s, two periodicals, *Ramparts* and *Evergreen Review* (*ER*), caused libraries and librarians to confront the censorship issue head-on. These confrontations illustrate the variety of ways libraries deal with controversy. In Los Angeles, the public library had to fight a city councilman's efforts to have *ER* removed from the library. The councilman was unsuccessful, but the library removed the current *ER* issues from public areas while the controversy raged. Eventually, the journal was returned to the open shelves after the parties reached a final decision. This was a short-term victory for censorship, but in the end, a victory for free access.

Not all librarians were so lucky. Richard Rosichan lost his position as director of the Kingston Area (New York) Public Library because he fought to keep *ER*, despite both library board and Johan Brich Society pressure to drop it. At the same time, the American Legion demanded that he remove *Ramparts* because of what the Legion considered its un-American stance. Groton (Connecticut) Public Library managed to retain its staff but lost its subscription to *ER*; after a four-month fight, the library's board of trustees ordered the removal of all issues from the library and the subscription cancelled. This was done under the threat of fines and jail sentences for both the library board and staff. Head librarian John Carey issued a statement to the effect that this decision would affect the general acquisition policy. One can only hope that he was wrong. Between keeping an item on the shelves and removing it is the compromise position to which librarians sometimes resort-restricted availability. The Philadelphia Free Library used this approach for *ER* when pressure began to be applied. The library renewed the subscription for the main building one under the age of 18 could examine the title.

Emerson Green away, who was at that time the director of libraries for the Philadelphia Free Library, said this was done because *ER* was "important sociological." Who was the winner here, the censor or the librarian?

Books

The list of books that have caused trouble over the years is immense. The short list included at the end of this section illustrates the range of titles while indicating that one can never really tell what will cause trouble. Some topics are more sensitive than others, and one might expect difficulty with certain acquisitions but not encounter any. However, sex, religion, and politics are always potential problems. Several school districts and public libraries faced complaints about *I Know Why the Caged Bird Sings* (Maya Angelou), because of passages dealing with child mole station and rape. In most instances, the objectors were successful of forcing its removal or restricting its use by requiring parental approval in writing. *The Adventures of Huckleberry Finn* (Mark Twain) has a long history of complaints. The complaints are a perennial problem. The usual charge is that the book contains racist material. Complaints are also frequently field over J.D. Salinger's *Catcher in the Rye*. Here the usual issue is profanity; occasionally, someone objects to sexual references. Another book that people claim contains inappropriate language is *One Hundred Years of Solitude* by Nobel prize-winner Gabriel Garcia Marquez. Other books draw complaints because of the point of view they present-for example, Dee Brown's *Bury My Heart at Wounded Knee.* Still others encounter problems for reasons that are hard to understand. Try to find the offending nudity in *Where's Waldo*? or determine why some school media centers have *Snow White* on the list of books that may be read only with signed parental approval.

According to an ACLU survey in 1997, the most frequently challenged authors between 1995 and 1997 were Judy Blume, Robert Cormier, Christopher Pike, and R. L. Stine. ALA's OIF indicated that the 1998 list of most challenged authors included all of the above, except Pike, and added Maya Angelou, James Lincoln Collier and Christopher Collier, Robie Harris, Lois Lowry, Katherine Paterson, and John Steinbeck.

One early 1999 case involved a Wisconsin school district's banning of four books dealing with gay themes-*When*

Someone You Know Is Gay, The Drowning of Stephen Jones, Body Be-Bop, and Two teenagers in Twenty. What is interesting about this case is that the complaint that led to banning was field by a parent of a former student in the school.

Music and Recordings

Though in the past there have been fewer problems with music than with other formats, that is no longer the case. Rap music, hard rock, and music lyrics in general now generate controversy quite regularly. In the late 1990s, 2 Live Crew recordings and performances draw national attention, and the concern continues to grow. Early in 1990, the recording industry instituted a labeling program similar to the motion picture rating system. This occurred after years of debate, even in Congress, and opposition from a variety of groups, such as the ALA. Anna Thompson's article, "Lyric Censorship," provides some good insights into this area. One older musical recording that still raises problems from time to time is *Jesus Christ, Superstar.* Some years ago, Rockford High School (Michigan) was the location of one such disagreement over both the music and the text. At the end of the debate, the school removed all materials relating to *Jesus Christ, Superstar* form the school system-both the library and the music department-because the musical was deemed "sacrilegious.

A good article that gives one a sense of how long people have been trying to censor music in the United States is Edward Volz's "You Can't Play That.

Games

Nothing in the collection is immune from challenge, as several libraries have learned the hard way. Aurora Public Library (Colorado) had to deal with controversy over *Dungeons and Dragons* (D&D) players' books. (D&D is a popular role-playing game with an estimated 3 million players, mostly young people.) A woman presented an official complaint and a petition with 150 signatures supporting the complaint. She claimed the game promotes "violence, Satanism and blasphemy of Christian terms." The complaint was withdrawn a short time later because the woman said she feared reprisals against her and her widowed mother. However, the publicity sparked a rash of complaints about other items in the library, and a local evangelist began checking area public library collections for D&D players' books. He tried to pursue the Aurora complaint, but because he did not live in the community, he could not file a complaint, At about the same time, in Hanover, Virginia, the parents of a 16-year-old who committed suicide sued a public school system.

The parents alleged that the suicide was a direct result of his playing D&D in a school building. Wrongful death lawsuits related to games, movies, and television programs have been increasing. None has involved libraries, but there is no reason to suppose that libraries will be immune from such a suit, particularly when many collections have materials about suicide. The November 1983 issue of *American Libraries* published some responses to the ALA Ethics Committee question, "Should you give a student a copy of *Suicide Mode D'Emploi*?" The book is said to be linked to at least 10 suicides. If one believes in freedom to read, what should one do?

Film and Video

As library collections of theatrical videos grow, so do the odds that some-one will demand the removal of one or more titles. Educational videos, especially those dealing with reproduction, abortion, and alternative lifestyles, also present problems. Even foreign-language videos, such as a Portuguese language film, can draw protests. During the Gulf War, some libraries rejected an antiwar video, raising the question of whether the librarians were acting as censors and not providing both sides of an issue. A short but informative article about issues of accessibility to video collections is by John Hurley.

LMU's large video collection has drawn several complaints. None of the challenges have been serious enough to warrant attention outside of the library, as no one from the university has raised the issue. To date, the complaints have been from community users who think the collection should only contain "Christian if not solely Roman Catholic" materials. Films such as *Jesus Christ, Superstar* and *The Last Temptation of Christ* have drawn highly negative comments from several community members. What might happen is a student's parents or major donor were to complain is difficult to say. We rather expect the issue would go beyond the walls of the library. Some years ago, librarians put on an amazing performance of self-censorship. The situation surrounding the film *The Speaker* includes almost every element one is likely to encounter in any censorship case. To fully understand all of the paradoxes that this event represents, one must review the background of the situation and view the film.

As with every other problem of this type, we have no objective data on which to base a judgment. Not all African Americans or other persons of colour who viewed the film saw it as racist. Just because one (albeit large) group claims that an item is this or that, does the claim make it so?

Is this really different from the Citizen's Committee for Clean Books saying that *The Last Temptation of Christ* is sacrilegious, or the John Brich Society claiming that

Ramparts and the *Evergreen Review* are anti-American? One hopes that most librarians will agree with Dorothy Broderick regarding *The Speaker*:

> Let librarians across the country decide for themselves: If they find the film boring, let them not buy it. If they feel that using it will stir up trouble in their community-as if they had invited "*The Speaker*"-let them ignore its existence. If the film is as bad as its opponents claim, it will die the natural death of an inadequate work in the marketplace.

Happily, the ALA has produced, or taken part in the production of, an excellent video, *Censorship us. Selection: Choosing Books for Public School.* 33 Though the focus is on public schools, the issues covered are broad enough to make the film valuable for use with any group to generate a discussion of intellectual freedom and censorship.

Special Cases

Sometimes there are unusual circumstances surrounding a book or other item of controversy, and there are major efforts to suppress the distribution of the item by governments of order groups. An extreme example was that of Salman Rushdie's *The Satanic Verses.* Although Rushdie was alive and still in hiding at this writing, several translators and publishers around the world who played some role in publishing of the book are dead. Bookstores stocking the book received threats, as did those involved in distribution of the book. To the best of our knowledge, no library received threats for adding the title to the collection. OCLC holdings statements in 1995, when there was still significant concern, showed that only 218 OCLC libraries held a copy. As of April 1999, a check of OCLC showed that 2,334 libraries held the title.

A good review article about the Rushdie situation and why *The Satanic Verses* was condemned is John Swan's "Satanic Verses, the Fatwa, and Its Aftermath," which describes the major events through mid-1991.

Librarians and Censorship

Basically, all the situations discussed so far are of the type that one can easily identify and choose to fight or not. Given the foregoing sample of the problems that one may encounter, it should not be surprising to find librarians acting in a self-protective manner. Will knowing who the most challenged authors are in some way influence selection decisions? How great a problem is this?

Several researchers have studied this phenomenon, but this discussion will explore the findings of only two of the more widely known studies, those of Fiske and Busha, and a recent study done a southern California. Marjorie Fiske shook the library profession some years ago when she reported that a high percentage of librarians decided not to buy an item because it might cause a problem. Some titles are likely to cause trouble, for example, *The Joy of Sex* or Madonna's Sex, and these are easy to identify. However, an examination of the sample list of titles that have caused trouble makes it evident that some problematic items are not easy to identify. After establishing the habit of not selecting a title that has the potential for controversy, it will be difficult to break the habit.

Unfortunately, as with so many other habits, it is easy to slip into a behaviour pattern without recognizing it. Reasons like "lack of funds," "no demand," or "poor quality" may be true, or they may be rationalizations for not selecting an item that might make life troublesome. Other excuses, such as "I will buy it when someone asks for it" or "I don't like that author or producer; he or she never has anything worth-while to say," clearly signal danger. Just because a librarian does not like an author or a subject does not mean that he or she has the right to keep others from access. This may not be self-protective in terms of one's own psyche. In any case, the result is the same-censorship.

One way to raise the level of self-awareness is to periodically check one's holdings against various lists of problem items. How many does the library have? Holdings of less than 50 percent should cause one to question what is happening in the selection process. There may be perfectly good reasons why there are so few of these items in the collection, but until the librarian can give good reasons, he or she cannot complacently say, "I am not a censor."

Charles Busha's study examined librarians' attitudes toward censorship and intellectual freedom. He compared his findings to scores on a standardized test that is an indirect measure of anti-democratic trends. His concluding sentence is probably a reasonable picture of all librarianship in the United States:

> It is evident, as a result of opinion research, that Midwestern public librarians did not hesitate to express agreement with cliches of intellectual freedom but that many of them apparently did not feel strong enough as professionals to assert these principles in the face of real or anticipated censorship pressures.

The data from a 1982 survey by Woods and Perry-Holmes indicated that the pattern of self-censorship continued, at least for small and medium-sized public libraries. A 1996 study of selection practices if five southern California public libraries suggested that little has changed since Fiske did her study more than 40 years ago.

It is pertinent to note that the dangers of censorship and having a commitment to avoid it is not enough in today's world. Information professionals must prepare for the censor long, long before there is a perceived threat or before the threat becomes real. The first step in preparing for the censor is to expect to have to face a censor. Prepare a policy statement about how the library will handle complaints, and have the policy approved by all the appropriate authorities.

There is nothing worse than having no idea of what to do when facing an angry person who is complaining about library materials. Even with policies and procedures, the situation may escalate into physical violence; without procedures, the odds of violence occurring increase. A typical procedure is to have the individual(s) file a formal complaint or fill out a form that specifies what is at issue of English, have recommended forms that are equally effective.

After the library develops the policies and procedures and they are approved, everyone working in public services needs to understand the system and receive training in implementing the system. (Sometimes role-playing is helpful in reinforcing the training.) ALA's Office for Intellectual Freedom has an excellent manual that provides details about what to do before censors arrive. Another good source is Frances Jones's *Defusing Censorship: The Librarian's Guide to Handling Censorship Conflicts.*

The ALA's organizational structure for dealing with intellectual freedom concerns is somewhat confusing. The Intellectual Freedom Committee (IFC) is responsible for making recommendations to the association regarding matters of intellectual freedom. The Office for Intellectual Freedom (OIF), which has a full-time staff, has the charge of educating librarians and others about intellectual freedom and censorship matters. It also is the support service for the IFC, and it implements the association's policies related to intellectual freedom. As part of its educational function, the OIF produces several publications: *Newsletter on Intellectual Freedom* (news and current developments relating to intellectual freedom), *QIF Memorandum* (addressed to local library association intellectual freedom committees), and the *Intellectual Freedom Manual.*

Filtering

Filtering access to the Internet has been a recent "hot topic" for the general public, government officials, and libraries. As we enter the twenty-first century, libraries appear to be "caught between a rock and a hard place" on this issue, as long as they offer Internet access to the public. Some of the general public, governing boards, and elected government officials want libraries to use filter software that will deny access to certain types of sites.

Others, believing in free speech (First Amendment), do not want filtering. The primary reason for filtering is to keep children from having access to "unacceptable" sites. An excellent article that describes how filtering works is Paul Resnick's article in *Scientific American.* Some of the cases involving libraries and filtering in 1999 reflect the problems that occur no matter which option is selected (filter or no filter). In Loudoun County, Virginia, the Public Library Board of Trustees adopted a policy in 1997 calling for the installation of filtering software on all public access computers that connected to the Internet. A citizens group (Mainstream Loudoun) filed suit against the board in 1998. Their basic argument was that (1) filters on all computers reduced everyone to the status of children, and

(2) filters cannot block access just to sites deemed inappropriate for children. (As an example of the limits on filtering, some filters would deny a person access to sites relating to breast cancer, because the word *breast* is considered a "stop" word.) Although the court held in favour of the plaintiffs in late November 1998,43 the board may appeal the decision. A former board member, now a Virginia state legislator, said he would introduce a bill that would require all public libraries to install filters.

Interestingly on the other side of the country the other side of the issue was also in court. The Pacific Justice Institute, an "organization dedicated to the defense of religious freedom", filed a lawsuit in 1998 against the city of Livermore, California, and its public library on behalf of a mother, because it did not have filtering software in place.45 According to the complaint, the woman's son had, on at least 10 occasions, downloaded images of nude women using library computers connected to the Internet. The suit was dismissed in January 1999, for the second time in a few months, on the basis that filtering was too restrictive of free speech and the right to receive free speech. Michael Millen, the attorney for the plaintiff, announced that he was appealing the decision.46 Thus, by mid-1999, there was no clear trend as to which way the issue will be decided.

The ALA prepared a statement about filtering in 1997. Not everyone in the ALA agreed with this statement, and by March 1999 there was some suggestion that ALA's policy might require modification. A meeting was held in March 1999 at ALA headquarters; it was a first-time meeting of filtering software producers and ALA officers and members to discuss the issue of filtering. Ann Symons, then ALA President, suggested that perhaps the IFC should reconsider the policy. A February 1999 *Library Journal* report on library filtering indicated that less than 20 percent of public libraries were using filtering software. How all these forces will play out is impossible to predict with any hope of accuracy. We suspect that by the time we prepare a new edition of this book, the issue will still be in the courts, as both sides challenge the presence or absence of policies or laws regarding access to the Internet and children.

Librarians frequently do not spend enough time learning about the circumstances in which reading or viewing may cause someone to harm a person or property. Perhaps a course or two in bibliotherapy should be required of any professional working in public service areas of a library or information center.

A standard definition of *bibliotherapy* is the "use of literature to bring about a therapeutic interaction between participant and facilitator." Some believe that a healing process takes place through reading, that is, that "thoughtful suggestions provide a reader with just the right book, a book that triggers a significant and growth producing feeling in response to some need." Most bibliotherapists operate on the basis of several assumptions:

- The process is interactive; it involves both participant and facilitator.
- Literature encompasses all forms of writing.
- The process is both clinical and developmental.
- The process can be one-on-one or group-based.
- The outcome is improved self-esteem and better assimilation of appropriate psychological or social values for the participant(s).

- The process is a therapy but draws heavily on the healthy aspects of the mind.
- The process depends on the facilitator's ability to select the appropriate material for the participant to read and consider.

There is much we do not know about reading or viewing and behaviour. Perhaps when we know more, our freedom-to-read statements may need revision. In many ways, the issues of filtering are rather like this as well. If we need to protect children from Internet materials, is it not also likely that we need to protect them from printed materials as well? *(Note:* it 15 not just about "protecting children from pornography," despite what some people say.)

Determining the effectiveness of bibliotherapy, or the effect or lack of effect of reading, viewing, and listening on behaviour, should be a high priority. The field makes the case for free and open access to all material for anyone at any time, yet there is some evidence that reading, viewing, and listening to certain items by certain people at certain times does affect behaviour in a positive or negative way.

The problem of censorship is complex, and it is necessary to do extensive reading and thinking about this topic. A theoretical example may help to illustrate just how complex the issue can be. Assume that a librarian is responsible for selecting materials for a small public library. Naturally, the librarian needs this job to cover living expenses. A small group of persons in the community wants the librarian to buy certain items for the library collection; but the librarian also knows of a large group of vocal and influential persons who would be upset, and might even demand that the librarian be fired, if the items were purchased.

Should the librarian buy the item and risk his or her family's welfare and own career over this? If the librarian does not buy the item, what can be said to the people who asked for its purchase? Does telling them they can get it somewhere else, or get it through interlibrary loan, really address that librarian's problem?

Appendices

APPENDIX–I

To: Responsible Administrative Officer

From: Librarian

Subject: Current Condition of the Library and Request for Detailed Study of the Library System.

This memorandum is a report on the condition of the library and the resulting problems affecting the efficiency of operations and realization of the library's ultimate goal of the best possible service to its users.

The purpose of this report is to request approval for a full analysis of the library's problems to determine the cost of correcting them and the cost of maintaining and improving on the resulting gains.

The analysis would be undertaken with the full cooperation of the present library staff which at the same time must maintain operations and services at the present level to the extent possible while supplying the data needed in the study. For this reason I believe a detailed survey and analysis requires the assistance of a systems analyst whose sole function would be to study the problems and recommend actions for the improvement of the library's operations and service. Therefore I also request approval for the appointment to the library staff of a qualified analyst to conduct the study under my direction.

The problems to be investigated and solved are suggested by the conditions described below. From routinely kept operating statistics and observation some of the conditions adversely affecting the library's operations and causing a continuous decline in its ability to serve the purposes for which it exists are listed.

1. Missing from the active book collection are 5,531 volumes which should be replaced.
2. The lesser used collection of 4,500 books has had to be stored in cartoons making the books inaccessible to users.
3. Approximately 1,000 volumes of books are in serious need of binding with another 3,000 requiring simple mending and relettering.
4. In the matter of the library's catalogue records:
   (*a*) The present shelf list is not a complete listing of the library's resources nor does it provide in many instances the accurate descriptive information necessary for the identification and location of the individual items in the collections.

   (*b*) Over 10,000 of the shelf list records are not unit cards but merely brief and incomplete records.

   (*c*) The shelf list card drawers are badly overcrowded.

   (*d*) The public catalogue is not a union catalogue of all library materials in the central and outlying collections.

   (*e*) There are many inconsistencies of filling in the public catalogue with neither the ALA or Library of Con-gress filing rules having been applied consistently.

   (*f*) The public catalogue record of multivolume holdings has not been kept up in many instances.

(*g*) Rules of entry for making personal and corporate name references in the public catalogue have not been followed in the majority of cases.

(*h*) The public catalogue files are overcrowded for efficient filling and convenient consultation.

5. In the matter of the library's serials or journal collection:

(*a*) More than 450 journal titles are incomplete—missing issues and volumes—largely traceable to lack of binding.

(*b*) Less than 30 per cent of the journal collection of 42,000 volumes is bound.

(*c*) Many unbound journals are beyond repair or binding and should be replaced or discarded.

(*d*) The majority of serials are only classified, not catalogued, resulting in incomplete information in the shelf list and main catalogue.

(*e*) Over 300 titles of monographs in series are classified in the serials collection, representing about 4,000 separate monographic titles unavailable to the user by author, title, editor, subject content and so forth.

6. In the matter of the library's ordering or acquisitions operations the backlog of user requests has increased to some 4,000 items with each month's report showing a 150 to 200 growth of this backlog. Under these circumstances unit processing costs continue to rise.

7. In the matter of the library's cataloguing operations:

(*a*) Cataloguing arrearage is now at 3,500 volumes and increasing monthly.

(*b*) Filing of the catalogue records cannot be kept up to date.

(c) Needed titles remain in the cataloguing department well over three months on the average awaiting receipt of Library of Congress catalogue card sets.

(*d*) Cataloguing processing is seriously slowed by use of the Dewey classification system, requiring reclassification of whole sections of older books as new editions of this classification schedule appear.

(*e*) Unit costs of cataloguing seem inordinately high and increasing with direct charges per unit cataloged in the range of $5.00 to $6.00.

8. In the matter of the library's reader services:

(*a*) User complaints are growing stemming largely from the delay in book ordering and cataloging.

(*b*) The library is impaired in its capability to participate in cooperative network services due mainly to the inadequacy and lack of standardization of its bibliographic records.

(*c*) The reader services staff is handicapped in providing services to our users as a result of the incomplete and inaccurate catalogue and other bibliographic records.

(*d*) Circulation records are in many instances not useful in identifying the location of materials out of the central collection due to the large number of missing books and those placed in inactive, inaccessible storage.

(*e*) Many user complaints are based on not finding materials reportedly in the collection. Many users report finding only one out of every three books they are seeking.

(*f*) Mutilation of journals and books is evident and the necessarily slow replacement of missing pages and issues is another source of user complaints.

9. In the matter of the branch libraries:

(a) Thirty-eight per cent of the central library book budget was spent in duplicating materials in the branch libraries during the past fiscal year.

(b) Various shelving, classification and cataloging schemes are employed by the branch libraries. Some do not maintain card catalogs or indexes of any sort.

(c) Circulation policies in the branch libraries are capricious. Certain ones allow books to circulate for various lengths of time with little if any follow-up procedure, while others allow no book check-out at all.

The existing condition of the library is the result of attempts over a period of years to satisfy the needs of our community with a limited operating budget and the consequent stop-gap measures. Many libraries today find themselves in this position and it appears to me that we would be shortsighted if we did not study our current problems and plan for the demands of the future by undertaking a total systems study.

The study should lead to establishing the interrelationships of operations and procedures could be designed that would solve the aforementioned problems as a whole rather than isolated solutions that of themselves are likely to create problems in other areas. A study may lead to an indication of the need for automation of the extensive data processing operations of a library. With our computer center it would seem logical to think of systems design in this context, whether for immediate implementation or in the future.

I believe the requested study would prepare the library to serve the immediate and long-range goals and objectives of our institution. I am aware that this proposal requires an extraordinary, appreciable expense but recommend this course as imperative to the development of the "good" library you envision.

Your authorization of a system study conducted by an analyst skilled in scientific management techniques is respectfully urged.

Should you require clarification, I am prepared to discuss in greater detail the generally stated condition of the library and the implications as I see it.

APPENDIX–II

HANDBOOK OF MANUAL PROCEDURE— ACQUISITIONS SYSTEM

1. Preorder Search Subsystem

   A. Book request received

      1. Check all given information provided on the request slip for completeness and spelling. If complete or can be readily completed, do so and continue; if not, return to requestor.

      2. Post record of the number of requests received on daily statistics sheets according to originating department.

   B. Is the request for a series? If yes, see No. 1 of this item B; if not, see No. 2 of this item B.

      1. If the request is for a series or part of a series (that is, a publication issued in successive parts and generally intended to be continued indefinitely), check the continuation card file in the acquisitions system and, if necessary, the central serials file in the serials system.

         (*a*) If the library receives the series, record the request as a duplication, indicating the call number; check the STANDING/ORDER box and return to the sender.

         (*b*) If not located, continue search in public catalogue.

      2. Search the public catalogue

         [The Dewey decimal catalogue, for material before 1996, and LC (Library of Congress) catalogue, beginning in 1966, are searched by main entry (author line) and/or by title, whichever the searcher feels is the more accurate approach. Place a check mark on the book purchase request form against the step taken, for example, check in boxes, OFF. CAT., PROOF CD, PUB. CAT., and so forth.]

(*a*) Is the book already in the library collection?

1. If the book is found to be in the collection and the request is not for an added copy, the call number is recorded on the request slip in the box, IN LIB LOC and CALL NO. The LIB HAS box is checked and the appropriate box on the side of the request slip is checked (PUB. CAT.). The request form is recorded on the daily statistics as a duplication by department and is returned to the request or.

2. If the request is for a departmental library and the book is found to be in that library, the DEPT HAS box is checked, the call number is recorded in the IN LIB LOC and CALL NO. box, and the request is recorded as a duplicate and returned to the requestor.

3. If the book is found in the collection and the request is for another copy for the general library or a departmental library, the call number is entered in the box, IN LIB LOC and CALL NO. In the LC CARD NO. box, "AC" (Added Copy) is recorded to indicate there is no need to order Library of Congress cards. The following information is verified and/or recorded on the request slip:

   (*a*) Official main entry (author line)

   (*b*) Publication date

   (*c*) Publisher and series note.

The appropriate boxes on the request slip are checked and the search is continued in the computer-produced "In Process" list, and, in *Books in Print* (BIP), the latter for ascertaining the price and the publisher.

(*b*) If the book is not in the library, the search is continued.

C. Search title in *In Process List*
(This computer-produced list contains books ordered and not received as well as books ordered and received but not cataloged. It is arranged alphabetically by title.)

1. If the title being searched is found in this list and is not a request for an added copy, it is considered a duplication and recorded on the statistics sheet by department, the ON ORDER box is checked, and the request slip is returned to the originator.

   (*a*) If the request is for an added copy, fill in box IN LIB LOC and CALL NO., enter "AC" in LC CARD NO. box, verify or correct author and title, and continue search in BIP.

2. If title is not found, continue search.

D. Search title in Library of Congress proofcard file

(file is alphabetical by title and located in the acquisitions system).

1. If appropriate card is found, take from file:

   (*a*) If necessary, correct main entry (author entry) on the request slip to conform with proof card.

   (*b*) If main entry on request slip differs from proof card, recheck the public catalogue and in process list if the search was made under a different entry. Also check the continuation file and, if necessary, the central serials file if a series note is now evident.

(*c*) Record LC card number and write "proof" in the LC CARD NO. box, to indicate that there is no need to order LC cards.

(*d*) Attach the LC proof card to request slip and continue the search for the price of the book.

2. If no LC proof card is located, continue search.

E. Search *Books in Print* (BIP bound cumulative volumes issued annually; approach is by subject, author, or title; this is an index to most domestic publishers' lists).

1. If entry is found, verify and/or record the following:

(*a*) Price

(*b*) Publication data

(*c*) Publisher

If all information necessary for ordering the book (namely, the library does not have, or order, or in process, and the author, title, LC card number, price, publisher, and publication data) is recorded on the request slip, the search is completed; give to the acquisitions librarian.

F. Search Forthcoming Books (FORTH. BOOKS)

(Bimonthly publication allowing approach by author and/ or title. Publication data to the month is included in entry.)

1. If entry is found, verify and/or record the following information:

(*a*) Price

(*b*) Publication data

(*c*) Publisher

With this information recorded, forward request to acquisitions librarian.

2. If not found, continue search.

G. Search request in domestic or foreign publishers' catalogs (PUBL. CAT.) and/or *Publisher's Trade List Annual* (PTLA is an annual bound compilation of American publishers' catalogs).

1. If located, verify an/or record the following information:

(*a*) Price

(*b*) Publication data

(*c*) Publisher

If all information needed to order is complete, forward to acquisitions librarian.

2. If not found, continue search.

H. Search *Publishers' Weekly* (PW; a weekly listing by author of new books) and/or *Book Publishers' Record* (BPR; a monthly cumulation of PW lists, classified by Dewey decimal numbers, with an author, title, and subject index).

1. If located, verify and/or record the following information:

(*a*) Price

(*b*) Publication data

(*c*) Publisher

2. If not found, continue search.

I. Search request in *Cumulative Book Index* [CBI; a cumulative world list of books in the English language; an author, title, or subject approach is possible; the LC card number is usually listed under the main (author entry].

1. If located, verify an/or record:

   (*a*) Main entry

   (*b*) LC card number

   (*c*) Publisher

   (*d*) Publication data

   (*e*) Price

   (*f*) Series note (If a new or different series note is discovered, check the continuation file and, if necessary, the central serials file.)

   With this information recorded, forward to acquisitions librarian.

2. If the main entry is different from that searched, begin search over again in public catalogue.

3. If not located, continue search.

J. Search in *National Union Catalogue* (NUC; an extensive set of volumes issued in various editions, containing retrospective cataloging data on most books and series to be found in the Library of Congress and other large research libraries; approach is by official main entry).

1. If found, verify and/or record the following information:

   (*a*) Publisher

   (*b*) Publication data

(*c*) LC card number

(*d*) Series note (If series note is found, check the continuation file and, if necessary, the central serials file.)

With this information recorded, forward request to acquisitions librarian.

2. If not located, place "XXX" in the LC CARD NO. box. Forward to acquisitions librarian.

K. Request reviewed by acquisitions librarian

1. Is there enough information to purchase book?

(*a*) If yes, send request to order subsystem.

(*b*) If no, either return to request or for additional information or to searcher for suggested alternative approaches and sources.

2. Is the book apparently out of print?

(*a*) If not, send request to order subsystem.

(*b*) If out of print (OP), notify request or and refer request slip to desiderata file in order subsystem.

Glossary

Administrative Metadata - Used for managing the digital object and providing more information about its creation and constraints governing its use. See also digital provenance administrative metadata, rights management administrative metadata, source administrative metadata, and technical administrative metadata.

AIP: Archival Information Package - The internal representation of an object into the Digital Preservation Repository, including all data generated upon ingest (e.g., descriptive metadata) needed to manage and preserve it.

Alternate Object Identifier - An optional unique identifier for an object supplied by the producer. Also known as a local identifier.

ARK: Archival Resource Key - A naming scheme for persistent access to CDL-hosted digital objects. An ARK is a specially constructed, actionable, and persistent URL encapsulating a globally unique identity that is independent of the current service provider. Each ARK is by definition bound to three things: object access, object metadata, and a faceted commitment statement about providing persistent access. With a single question mark (?) appended, an ARK connects users to the object's metadata; with a doubled question mark (??), it connects to the provider's commitment statement. See the ARK web site for more information.

Authorized Signator - The person designated by the producer as having signature authority for contracts and legal agreements. This person signs the submission agreement.

Behaviors Metadata - Metadata used to associate executable behaviors with content in the METS object. A behavior section has an interface definition element that represents an abstract definition of the set of behaviors represented by a particular behavior section. A behavior section also has a behavior mechanism which is a module of executable code that implements and runs the behavior sdefined abstractly by the interfact definition.

Citation Linker - An Ex Libris SFX tool that allows linking from a citation to the full text of an item, or to other services (such as Request for interlibrary borrowing). While used primarily for interlibrary loan, it can also be used to facilitate the location of citations by researchers.

Commitment Statement - A declaration by an organization of its intention to retain and make available a given object or set of objects. This may include such things as the length of time an object identifier will be valid and how invariant the object's content will be.

Complex Digital Object - Includes two or more content files (and their format variants or derivatives) and corresponding metadata. The content files are related as parts of a whole and are sequenced logically, such as pages. For example, a complex digital object could consist of a multi-page diary scanned as TIFF images, from which are generated display images (JPEGs and GIFs), plus a transcription of the diary and the metadata for each file. See also digital object, simple digital object.

Component - Content file or a metadata package that is part of a digital object.

Content File - A file that is either born digitally or produced using various kinds of capture application software. Audio, image, text, and video are the basic kinds of content files. Versions of a content file may be dispersed across several file formats. For example, an image may be scanned into a TIFF file and then JPEG and GIF files may be created from the TIFF file to increase delivery speeds and protect property rights.

Crawl - The activity of using software to recursively download web documents by following links. There are a variety of crawl methods, including: focused crawl, smart crawl, incremental crawl, targeted crawl, and customized crawl. See also crawler.

Crawler - Also known as a spider or robot. Software that automatically traverses the web by downloading documents and following links from page to page. See also crawl.

CrossRef - A collaborative reference linking service. See the CrossRef web site for more information.

Customized Crawl: Application Programming Interface - A web crawl optimized for a particular web site based on human knowledge of the structure and content of the site.

Data Content Standard - Rules for determining and

formulating data values within metadata elements. Examples include the Anglo-American Cataloging Rules (AACR), Cataloging Cultural Objects (CCO), Describing Archives: a Content Standard (DACS), and Graphic Materials (GIHC).

Data Interchange Standard - Used to define the encoding, storage, transmission, and interchange of data values represented within a data structure standard. Examples include the Dublin Core RDF/XML, MODS, and MARC21 formats.

Data Structure Standard - Standards that define metadata elements. Examples of data structure standards include Dublin Core, MODS, and MARC21.

Data Value - A discrete unit of data within a metadata element, i.e., the data encoded within a tag.

Data Value Standard - Data value standards govern the choice and form of controlled forms of data values within metadata elements. These controlled data values are often found in the form of thesauri, vocabulary lists, and authority files. Examples include the Library of Congress' Subject Cataloging Manual (SCM) and the Art & Architecture Thesaurus (AAT) rules.

Deep Web - Consists of materials that are available by HTTP and are publicly available, but are not included in standard public indexes such as Google. This includes materials that are difficult or impossible to crawl, such as databases.

Descriptive Metadata - Metadata used for the discovery an dinterpretation of the digital object. Descriptive metadata may be referred to externally or indirectly by pointing from the digital wrapper to a metadata object, a MARC record, or an EAD instance located elsewhere. Or, descriptive metadata may be embedded in the appropriate section of the digital wrapper.

Digital Assets - A collection of computer files that contain intellectual content (images, texts, sounds, video) and/or descriptive metadata of the content and its digital format. They represent an investment for the depositor and an information resource for the researcher.

Digital Object - An entity in which one or more content files and their corresponding metadata are united, physically and/or logically, through the use of a digital wrapper. See also complex digital object, simple digital object.

Digital Object Production - The process by which the content file(s) and corresponding metadata are united in the digital wrapper, i.e., MoA II; XML DTD, or METS. The process may be accomplished manually, or it may be automated to increasing degrees using spreadsheets and database applications.

Digital Preservation - The managed activities necessary for ensuring the long-term retention and usability of digital objects.

DPR Administrator - A Digital Preservation Repository staff member who serves as proxy and performs administrative functions, such as registration and updates.

DPR Designated Community - The University of California libraries that may deposit content in the Digital Preservation Repository.

Digital Provenance Administrative Metadata - Administrative metadata that is the history of migrations, transformations, or translations performed on a digital library object's content files from their original digital capture or encoding. It should contain information regarding the ultimate origin of the content files.

Digital Wrapper - A structured text file that binds digital object content files and their associated metadata together and that specifies the logical relationship of the content files. METS is an emerging, XML-based international standard for wrapping digital library materials. All of the content files and corresponding metadata may be embedded in the digital wrapper and stored with the wrapper. This is physical wrapping or embedding. Or, the content files and metadata may be stored independently of the wrapper and referred to by file pointers from within the wrapper. This is logical wrapping or referencing. A digital object may partake of both kinds of wrapping.

Dim Archive - An archive that is inaccessible to the public, but that can easily be made accessible if required. It's typically used for the preservation of content that is accessible elsewhere. See also dark archive, light archive.

Drop-Down Menu - A selection field that only displays one choice at first; the list box is hidden until the user expands it by clicking on it with the mouse or some other action. It is not the same thing as a pull-down menu.

Dublin Core - A simple set of metadata elements used as a common meeting ground between richer, more granular metadata standards from diverse groups. Allows for generalizability and the support of cross-collection discovery. See the Dublin Core Metadata Initiative (DCMI) web site for more information.

Element - A discrete component of metadata, or a discrete component of a data structure defined by a DTD or schema (often represented through markup in the form of a tag).

Emulation - The imitation of a computer system, performed by a combination of hardware and software, that allows programs to run between incompatible systems. Or, the ability of a program or device to imitate another program or device.

Finding Aid - A guide or inventory to a collection held in an archive, museum, library, or historical society. It provides a detailed description of a collection, its intellectual organization and, at varying levels of analysis, of individual items in the collection.

Focused Crawl - A web crawl designed to download online documents within specific parameters, such as file type, size, or location. The crawler follows only certain kinds of links and ignores others. Examples: a crawl might focus on HTML and PDF files and ignore sound and video files. Or, a crawl might focus on one domain and not follow any links outside of that domain.

Full-Text Harvest - The harvest of text from target pages to build a full-text index with links to the target resources. This is the same thing Google and other search engines do when performing a search.

Incremental crawl - Designed to update a previous crawl. Evaluates web pages and documents based on previous crawls and downloads only those that have had changes, additions, and deletions.

Ingest - The process by which a digital object or metadata package is absorbed by a different system than the one that produced it.

Inside CDL - The web site primarily for UC library staff that provides access to the working documents of the CDL.

Inventory - A set of digital objects to be ingested into the Digital Preservation Repository. The objects will be submitted on behalf of a producer according to the terms of an inventory definition.

Inventory Definition - A document signed by both the producer and Digital Preservation Repository staff that describes an inventory and records the negotiated data model, profile, rights agreements, and transmission method.

Light Archive - An archive that is accessible to the public. See also dim archive and dark archive.

Link - A URL that references resources integral to the digital object. In some instances, these references may be to internal parts of the object (e.g., another sub part of the overall digital object). In other instances, these references may be to resources that exist outside and independent of the digital object but that are, nevertheless, an important part of the digital object's content.

Link Resolver - Software that brings together information about the cited resource, the user, and the library's many subscriptions, policies, and services. For the software to work, the content providers must be willing to participate as sources (databases or sites that can provide a link from a reference). The link resolver becomes activated when the user clicks on a link or button ("Search for full text") embedded in the user interface of PubMed (or other services). Using the OpenURL framework, information is bundled together from the source and sent to the resolver software that will process the data and compare it to the Knoweldgebase. The user is then presented with a range of options for locating the article, such as a link to the online article or journal, a listing for the library's print holding for that title, interlibrary loan, or document delivery options.

Lot Identifier - A Digital Preservation Repository identifier for a set of digital objects that were submitted during a specific time period.

Metadata - Structured information about an object, a collection of objects, or a constitutent part of an object such as an individual content file. Digital objects that do not have sufficient metadata or become irrevocably separated from their metadata are at greater risk of being lost or destroyed. Ephemeral, highly transient digital objects will often not require more than descriptive metadata. However, digital objects that are intended to endure for long periods of time require metadata that will support long-term preservation. See also administrative metadata, behaviors metadata, descriptive metadata, file inventory metadata, and structural metadata.

Metadata Harvest - The harvest of existing metadata records from resource repositories, such as through OAI, to gather metadata for query results or index creation.

Metasearching - The act of searching more than one database simultaneously through the use of metasearch software. Also called "cross-database searching" or "federated searching."

Migration - The transfer of digital objects from one hardware or software configuration to another, or from one generation of computer technology to a subsequent generation. The purpose of migration is to preserve the integrity of digital objects; and to retain the ability for clients to retrieve, display, and use them in the face of constantly changing technology. Migration includes refreshing as a means of digital preservation, however, it is not always possible to make an exact digital copy of a database or other information object and still maintain the compatibility of the object with a new generation of technology.

Mirroring - The process of making exact replicas of resource items, such as web pages, with slight modifications to hyperlinks as needed to reproduce the behavior of the items. This is similar to using the "save as" function from a browser to save a local copy of the page, including its contents and images.

Object Identifier - The primary identifier for a digital object within the Digital Preservation Repository, usually an ARK.

OpenURL - An academic unit established by UC to provide a supportive infrastructure for interdisciplinary research complementary to the academic goals of departments of instruction and research.

Participatory Metadata Harvest - The harvest of implicit metadata, text, and format information from items to create metadata. For example, during a web crawl, a web page could be fed into an automated metadata harvest engine, such as PhraseRate, to create a title, author, description, and keywords based on document formatting and key phrase repetitions.

Portal - A web site or service that provides access to online resources, such as digital objects.

Pre-Submission - A one-time process of information gathering and negotiation between the producer and Digital Preservation Repository staff regarding the possible ingest of a set of objects. This process usually culminates in the signing of a submission agreement and an inventory definition.

Pre-Submission Worksheet - A form filled out by the producer during pre-submission that provides information for Digital Preservation Program staff detailing licensing (rights information) and specifying the number of files, formats, metadata information, and delivery type.

Producer - An organization with legal, financial, and curatorial control over one or more object inventories to be submitted to the Digital Preservation Repository.

Producer Technical Contact - A person acting on behalf of the producer who manages the process (including the technical details) of submitting objects to the Digital Preservation Repository.

Pull-Down Menu - A menu that expands downward when its title is selected with the mouse. A list of options appears as long as the mouse button is held down, and the user can select an option by scrolling through the menu and releasing the mouse button when the desired option is highlighted (as defined by the

ComputerUser High-Tech dictionary). A pull-down menu is different than a drop-down menu.

Schema - A common way of defining the structure, elements, and attributes that are available for use in a XML document that complies to the schema.

Security Backup - A second copy of a set of digital assets made to protect against loss due to unintended destruction or corruption of the primary set of digital assets. Security backups are created routinely and are not to be considered archives.

SFX - The link server from Ex Libris that allows context-sensitive linking between web resources in the scholarly information environment. SFX accepts an OpenURL as input from an information resource, which is referred to as an SFX source. See the SFX web page for more information.

Smart Crawl - A focused crawl based on dynamic criteria. For example, a crawler could be programmed to analyze and evaluate a web site for volatility, the presence of metadata, or the structure and content of a site, etc. The more it crawls, the smarter it gets about what to crawl and what not to crawl.

Standard Access - A general access path provided by the CDL and the OAC, namely the OAC database. Customized access or portal to the depositor's digital assets is the responsibility of the depositor and not the CDL or the OAC.

Structural Metadata - Metadata used to indicate the logical or physical relationship of the content files comprising the complex digital object, e.g., the sequence of pages for a group of images of a diary or of detailed images of a larger image. The structural metadata spécifies a coherent presentation of the digital content and its pertinent associated metadata.

Submit - The act of transmitting a prepared digital object for deposit into the Digital Preservation Repository. Objects are prepared in accordance with the submission agreementand the CDL Guidelines for Digital Objects.

Submitter - A person or client system authorized by the producer to submit objects to the Digital Preservation Repository. A submitter also has the rights of a consumer.

Submission Agreement - A legal document through which the producer grants the Digital Preservation Repository the right to electronically store, convert, and copy digital assets for preservation purposes.

Surface - Includes materials that are publicly available by HTTP, are easily discoverable by crawlers, and are indexed by public indexes such as Google. Sometimes referred to as the static web. The opposite of the deep web.

Tag - A short, formal name used to indicate data structure or metadata elements, such as (title) in HTML or (unittitle) in EAD.

Targeted Crawl - A web limited to particular web sites based on desired content (compare to a focused crawl. A targeted crawl may or may not be customized.

Technical Administrative Metadata - Administrative metadata that describes the technical attributes of the digital file.

User - A login identity used to authenticate a person or client system as a submitter consumer, or administrator for an inventory.

Validation - A process to check one or more aspects of a submission for schema errors, file format problems, and ingest parameter inconsistencies that might affect its suitability for preservation. Results of a validation may include any combination of structural analysis information, warning messages, or fatal errors that prevent an object from being ingested.

Web Analyzer - A tool that gathers web metrics and background information about a particular web site to inform administrative, technical, and selection decisions about the capture, curation, and preservation of the digital entities. For example, an analyzer might provide information about the diversity of file formats, the size of the files, an idea about the content, and a comparison to content already captured. With this information, the potential costs, value of the content, and preservation strategy could be determined.

XSLT: eXtensible Stylesheet Language Transformations - Can be used to transform an XML document into another form such as PDF, HTML, or even Braille. XSLT stylesheets work as a series of templates that produce the desired formatting effect each time a given element is encountered. One of the most common uses of XSLT is to apply presentational markup to a document based on rules relating to the structural markup. For example, each time a "title" appears in the structural markup, the text within the element could be put into italics. XSLT can also control the order in which elements and attributes are displayed. This means that tables of contents or indexes can be generated automatically on the basis of the content of a document.

Bibliography

Britt, B. "What Thou Lovest Well Remaindered". *Small Press* 10 (Winter 1991): 52-55.

Carter, R. A. "Taking Aim at the Library Market". *Publishers Weekly* 237 (June 8, 1990): S6-S12.

Dan Ancona, Jim Frew, Greg Jan?e, and Dave Valentine. Accessing the alexandria digital library from geographic information systems. In *Proceedings of the Fourth ACM/IEEE-CS Joint Conference on Digital Libraries*, 2004.

Dave, R. *The Private Press*. 2d ed. New York: R. R. Bowker, 1983.

Eytan Adar and Jeremy Hylton. On-the-fly hyperlink creation for page images. In *Proceedings of the Second Annual Conference on the Theory and Practice of Digital Libraries*, 1995.

Finn, M. "Everything You Need to Know About Trademarks and Publishing". *Pub-lishers Weekly* 239 (January 6, 1991): 41-44.

Graham, G. "Publishers, Librarians and the Eternal Triangle". *Library Acquisitions: Practice and Theory* 15, no. 3 (1991): 261-64.

Grannis, C. B. *What Happens in Publishing?* 2d ed. New York: Columbia University Press, 1967.

Greco, Albert N. *The Book Publishing Industry*. Boston: Allyn & Bacon, 1997.

Hoffert, B. "Getting Published". *Library Journal* 115 (February 15, 1990): 153-56.

Hunter, K. A. "Making the Commercial Transition from Paper to Electronic: Or Pub-lishing in the 'Twilight Zone.'" *Collection Management* 15, nos. 112 (1992) 129-39.

Kenneth M. Anderson, Aaron Andersen, Neet Wadhwani, and Laura M. Bartolo. Metis: Lightweight, flexible, and web-based workflow services for digital libraries. In *Proceedings of the Third ACM / IEEE-CS Joint Conference on Digital Libraries*, 2003.

Kopka, M. "Backlist: How to Use It". *Publishers Weekly* 240 (October 4, 1993): 24-25.

Loe, M. K. H. "Book Culture and Book Business: U.K. vs. the U.S". *Journal of Academic Librarianship* 16 (March 1990): 4-10.

Mark S. Ackerman. Providing social interaction in the digital library. In *Proceedings of the First Annual Conference on the Theory and Practice of Digital Libraries*, 1994.

Newlin, B. "Traveling the New Information Superhighway". *Small Press* 12 (Spring 1994): 26-29.

One Book Five Ways. Los Altos, Calif.: William Kaufmann, 1977.

Paul S. Adler and Terry Winograd, editors. *Usability : turning technologies into tools.* Oxford University Press, 1992.

Posel, N. R. "High Priced or Over-Priced They're Every Library's Problem". *Reference Librarian* 19 (1987): 257-67.

R. Acuff, L. Fagan, T. Rindfleisch, B. Levitt, and P. Ford. Lightweight, mobile e-mail for intra-clinic communication. In *Proceedings of the 1997 AMIA Annual Fall Symposium*, pages 729-33, Oct 1997.

Reka Albert, Albert-Laszlo Barabasi, and Hawoong Jeong. Diameter of the World Wide Web. *Nature*, 401(6749), September 1999.

Rettig, J. "Do Publishers Have Ears?" *Wilson Library Bulletin* 62 (January 1988) 15-22.

Robert B. Allen and Jane Acheson. Browsing the structure of multimedia stories. In *Proceedings of the Fifth ACM International Conference on Digital Libraries*, 2000.

Robert B. Allen. A multi-timeline interface for historical newspapers. In *Proceedings of the Fifth ACM / IEEE-CS Joint Conference on Digital Libraries*, 2005.

Salace, J. "Video Distribution: The Maze Made Manageable". *Library Journal* 115 (July 1990): 42-44.

Sexton, M. "Replacing the Myths About Marketing to Libraries". *Publishers Weekly* 236 (March 10, 1989): 56-57.

Taylor, S. A. "Joys of Electronic Togetherness". *Publishers Weekly* 240 (March 29, 1993): 24-28.

Virgilio Almeïda, Azer Bestavros, Mark Crovella, and Adriana de Oliveira. Characterizing reference locality in the www. In *Proceedings of PDIS'96: The IEEE Conference on Parallel and Distributed Information Systems*, 1996.

Weisberg, J. "Rough Trade: The Sad Decline of American Publishing". *New Republic* 204 (June 17, 1991): 16-21.

William Y. Arms. Key concepts in the architecture of the digital library. *D-Lib Magazine*, Jul 1995.

Index